AF539263

No One Sees Me

David Sleppy

ISBN 978-1-60402-654-2

Cover and text design by design in bloom, inc

Printed and bound in China

Acknowledgments

I need to thank my mother, Margie, for giving me the desire to create, my father, Ernie, for lending me his free spirit and my stepfather, Bill, for teaching me enough discipline to be able to use those gifts.

Annamarie, your insight was invaluable and Jim, Pat and Carol, I am grateful for your encouragement.

Heidi, your editing was essential and thank you, Karen, for making the concept beautiful.

Foreword

David Sleppy was in downtown Toronto on a cold November day when he saw a young man sleeping on a sidewalk grate for its warmth. He could not help but wonder whose son this was. A month later, in Indianapolis, a homeless man expressed his concern that David did not have a coat. With these two experiences, a journey began, one that would take David from East Coast to West, and from Chicago to New Orleans, photographing the people of the street and learning some of their stories.

Asked about the hardest part of being homeless, one person replied, "No one sees me." This book is devoted to helping them be seen.

My experience with the homeless began in the mid '70s when I was supervising a restaurant on Vine Street in downtown Lexington, Kentucky. Particularly in the winter, they would come in the restaurant to try to find something to eat, to see if we would give them something, to warm up. The more ingenious of them would get a free cup of hot water and some ketchup packets... tomato soup.

As in many cities, trash was taken to the curb each night to be picked up. This became a staple for many of these people.

Our restrooms were their locker rooms. A place to be warm. A place to wash up. A place for them to be safe.

I let them stay as long as I thought reasonable considering the attitudes of our paying customers. But eventually, I would ask each of them to leave. And the homeless would go, shuffling off in the darkness to who knew where? I was never challenged by them, never a harsh word from them. I would imagine they had been asked to leave many places for the benefit of the more respectable patrons who did not want to share their space with these people... these souls who share the same one spirit we all share.

That restaurant on Vine Street in Lexington, Kentucky closed many years ago. The homeless are still on Vine Street.

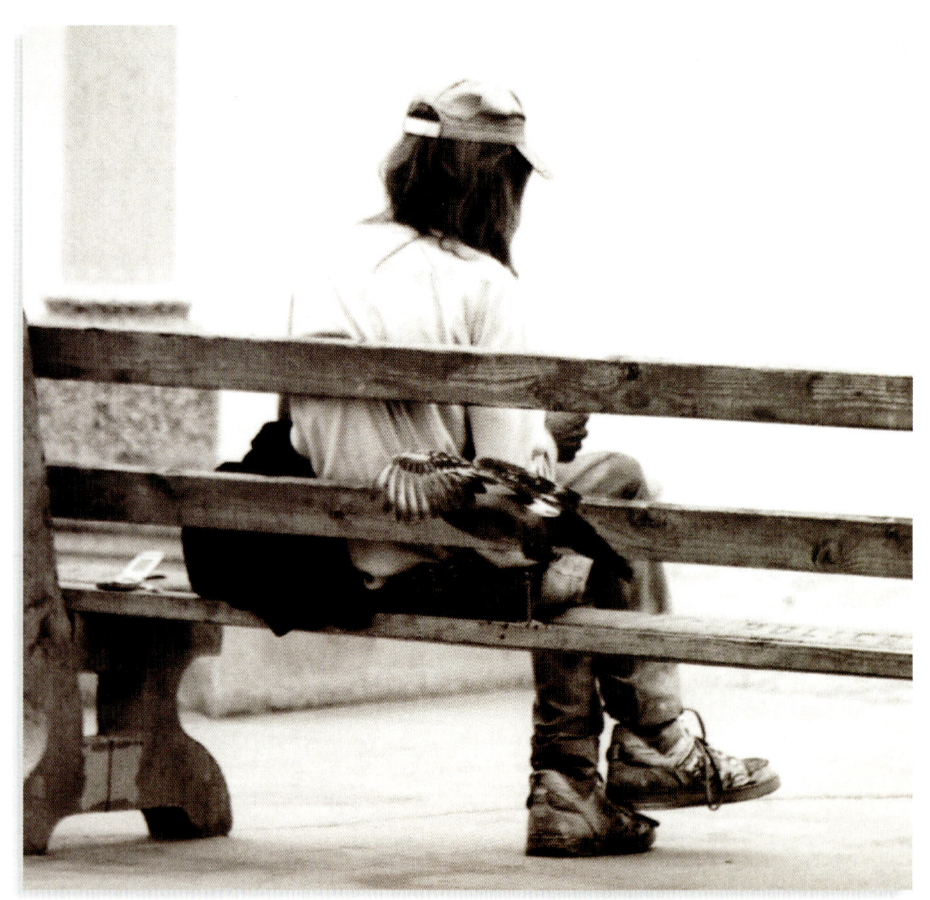

SANTA MONICA, CALIFORNIA

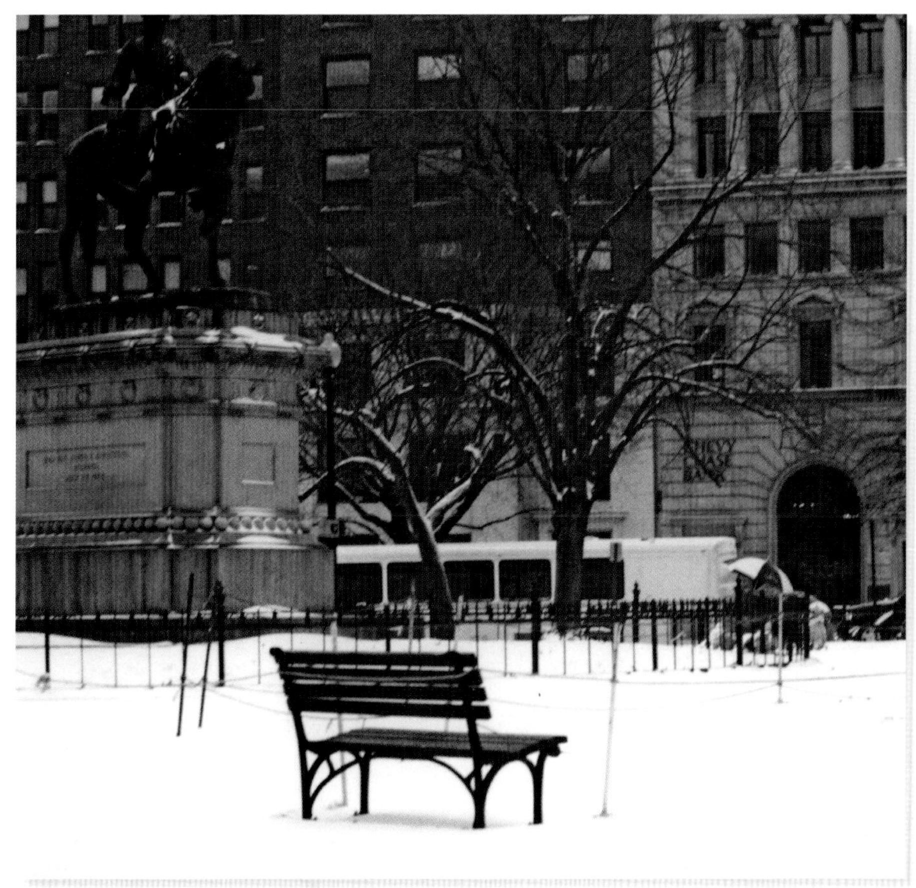

WASHINGTON, D.C.

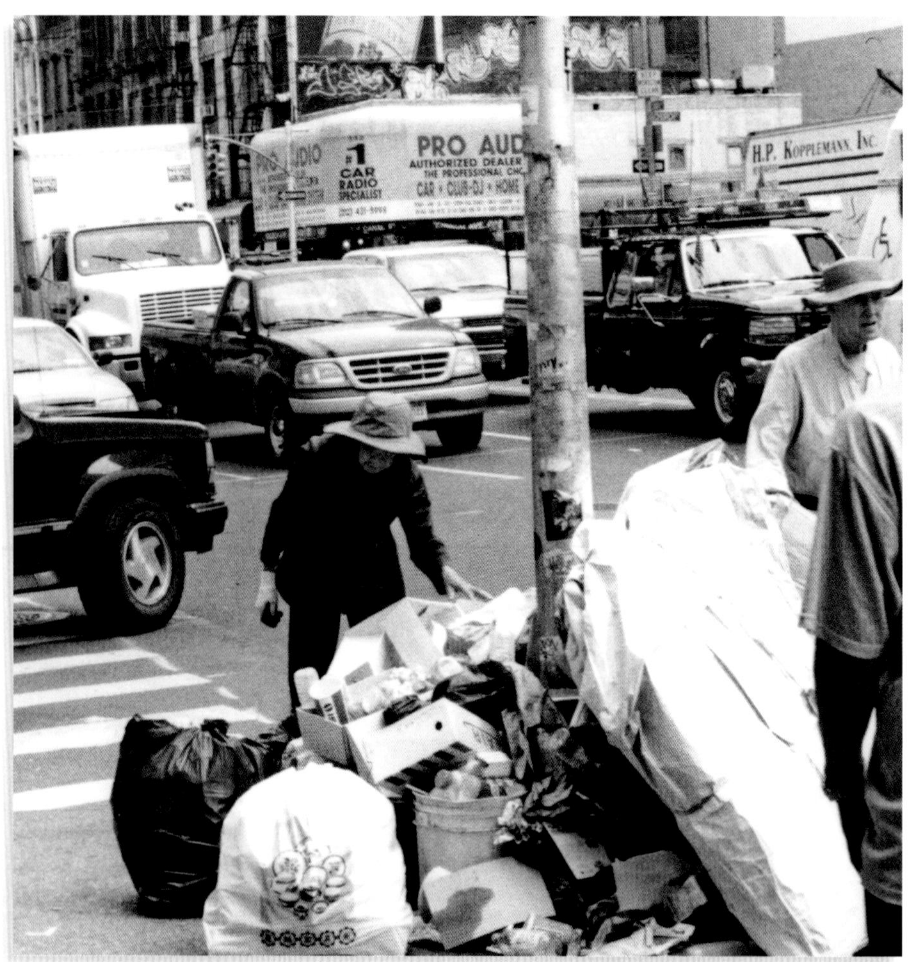

SOHO, NEW YORK

2003

It was two weeks before Christmas and I had just purchased the last gift, a bright red Kate Spade handbag for a friend. We had been browsing in this upscale department store a couple of weeks before and she had commented on the purse.

While I was happy with the gift and the fact my Christmas shopping was finished, as I walked through the store I couldn't help but feel a little sad, lonely. I remembered a small wine and cheese shop in the mall and I decided to see what pleasures the market might hold for me.

The store smelled of fresh-baked bread and one wall displayed hundreds of vintages, from every winemaking region of the world. The clerk was discussing the attributes of a particular merlot with two men in suits and I was able to hear his glowing description of the 1997 grapes from that vineyard. It sounded good to me and I bought a bottle, with the cashier wrapping it in purple tissue paper and then placing it in a white gift bag with a gold seal. Nice presentation for a bottle of wine.

I walked through the mall in the direction of the garage. I observed the people as they went about their lives. People laughing. People hurrying. People holding hands. People together. Only I was alone this Monday evening.

As I reached my car in the garage, I pressed the remote switch and the trunk of the Lincoln opened to receive the Christmas gift and the bottle of fine merlot. It was a fairly nice December evening so I decided to take a walk outside before going home to my empty house. I debated whether to take my coat, but thought instead the sweater I had on would be warm enough for tonight's mild weather.

In my neighborhood a tall black man lives in the second house on the left from the entrance. Every time he was in the front yard and I'd drive by, he would wave and flash me a huge smile. After a year of this, I stopped and introduced myself. His name is Willy.

I saw the exit of the garage and headed outside. I walked past restaurants and shop windows, all decorated for Christmas. I began to get a little chilly and stuck my hands deep in the pockets of my khaki pants. It was night now and as I turned the corner on the way back to my car, the wind struck my face. I put my head down against it.

As I approached the garage entrance, I heard a hearty voice. "Hey, it can't be that bad," the man called. I looked up and saw Willy about twenty feet away, looking at one of the beautifully decorated department store windows. I approached him with a smile, my hand out to shake his, happy to find someone I knew. "How are you?" I asked. But as we shook hands, I realized it wasn't Willy. The hands of this tall black man were hard and dry, cracked. He responded to my question with one of his own, concerned. "Don't you have a coat?" he asked. I replied that yes, I had a coat.

I didn't quite know what to do, what to say to the stranger. Then he began to talk. "I have lost my place to sleep in all this rain we've had lately," he said. I asked what he meant. "Well, I was sleeping down there." He pointed to the south, where there was a railroad bridge. "But the rain ruined my cardboard box and the wind blew away the piece of plastic I had. I've tried to get a job, but no one is hiring."

I asked what kind of work he did and he replied he was a cook. He said that one restaurant told him they would hire him after the first of the year, but not now.

I looked at him. He was clean, dressed in a baseball hat and a down jacket. He was shaved. I listened to him. He spoke well. He asked for nothing. He was concerned about my mood, my well-being, my not wearing a coat. But his cardboard box was ruined, his plastic cover blown away.

I reached in my pocket, pulled out a twenty dollar bill, and handed it to him discreetly. I told him to take care of himself and turned to walk away. He called for me to wait. "Are you a prayerful man?" he asked. I told him I was, although in my mind I noted I didn't pray as much as I used to. "I have nothing to give you but a prayer. Will you pray with me?" I nodded and he took my hand in both of his. I felt awkward, but stood still.

"Lord," he prayed, "bless this man who has helped me tonight... don't let anything bad happen to him tonight and please don't let anything bad happen to me tonight either. Amen." He let go of my hand and we nodded and walked away in opposite directions.

His was a true Christmas gift... he had only a prayer and he shared it with me.

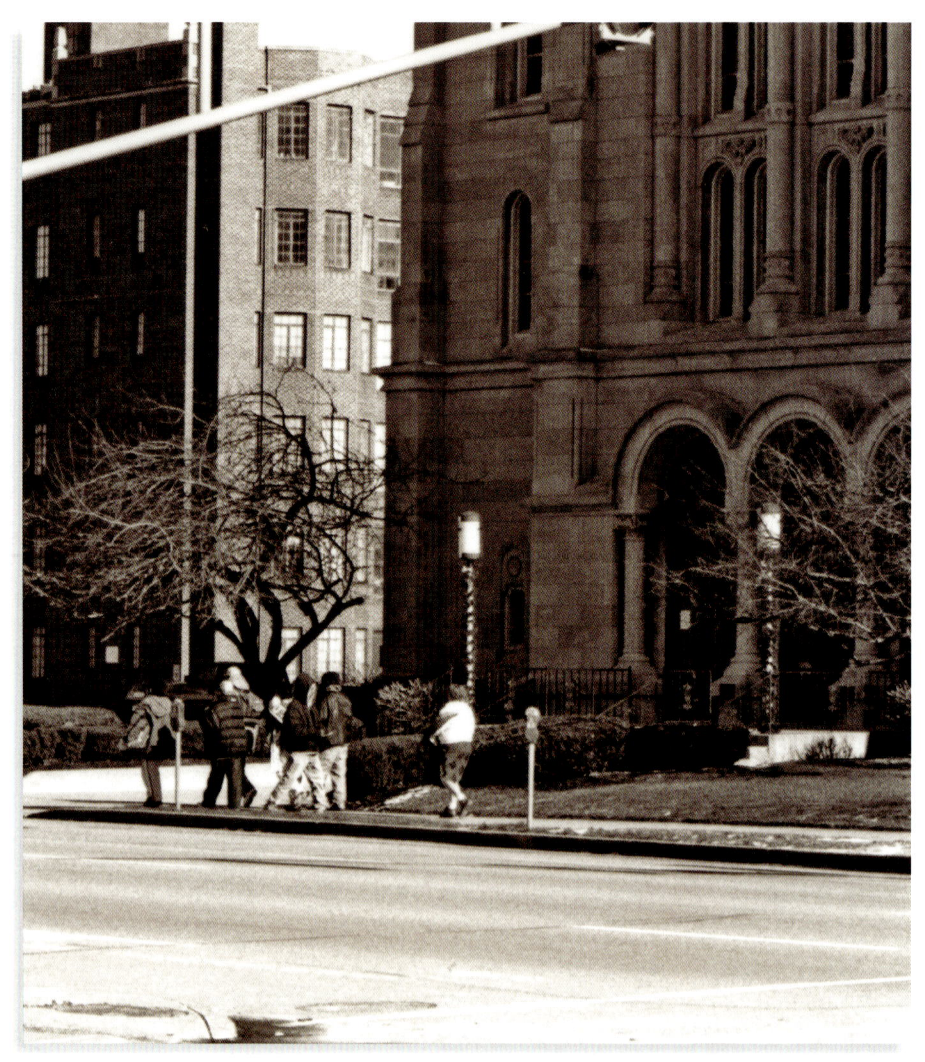

INDIANAPOLIS, INDIANA

Christmas Day, 2003.

Downtown Indianapolis was quiet on Christmas Day. There were very few people on the streets, even though it was a pleasant enough day for that time of year.

Driving down Pennsylvania Avenue, I began to notice a stream of people, mostly men, carrying plastic bags that obviously had items in them they were pleased to have. Then I noticed a steady line of other people headed in the opposite direction, apparently toward the place where the plastic bags were available.

I parked my car a couple of blocks away and fell in with those going to receive their windfall of Christmas items. They led me to a church and we went inside. Like those in front of me, I was offered a laminated ticket for a meal and invited to go downstairs to eat. I would have been the 171st lunch served on that Christmas Day.

Thank you, Rosie.

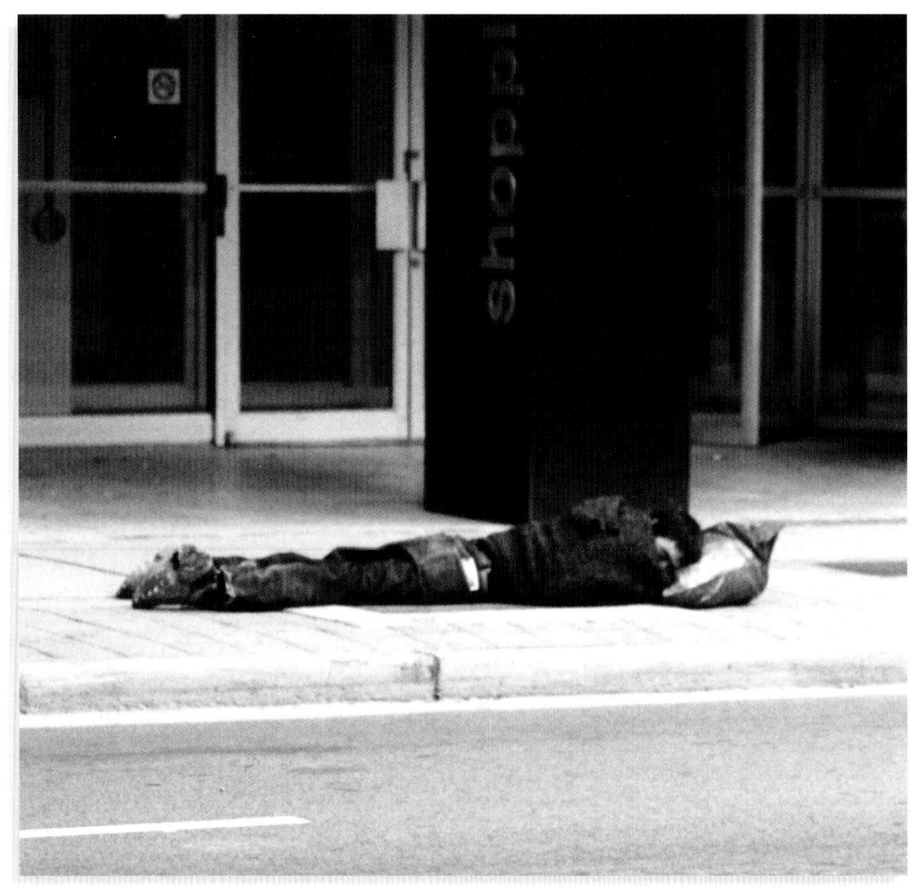

WHOSE SON IS THIS?

TORONTO, CANADA

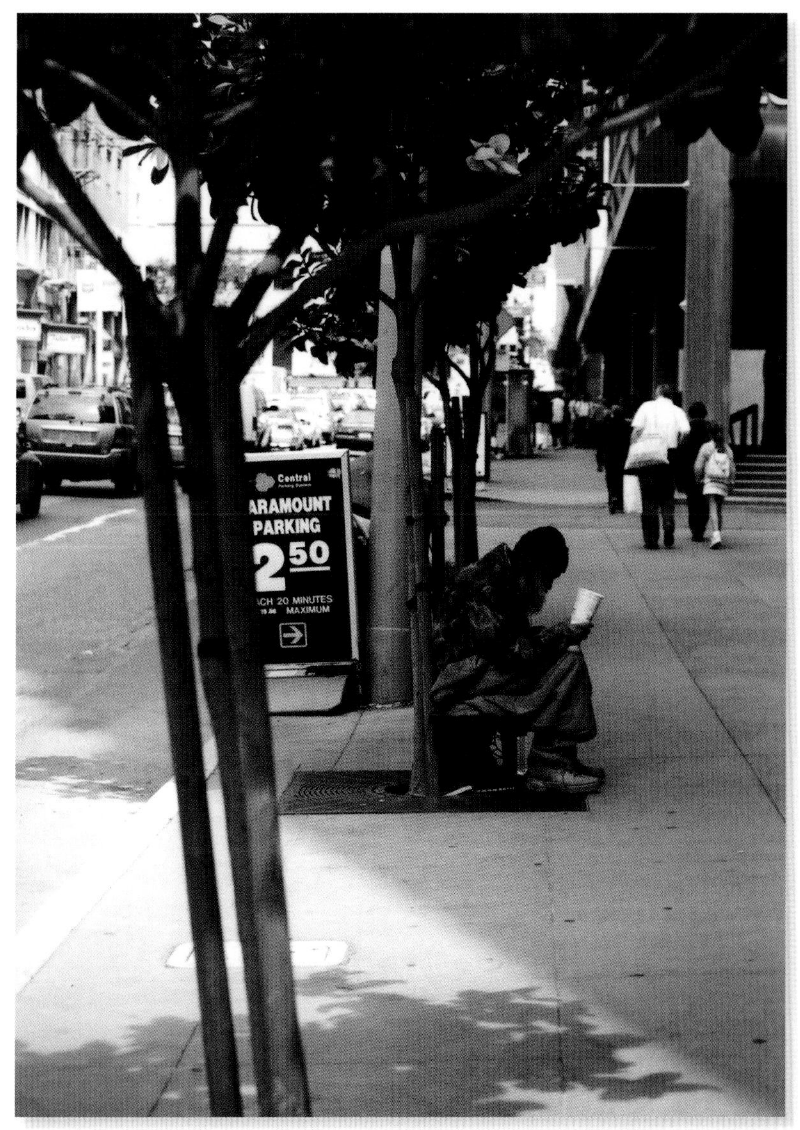

$2.50 to park. For 20 minutes.

Has he paid to park here? Probably so.

Probably more than we can imagine.

San Francisco, California

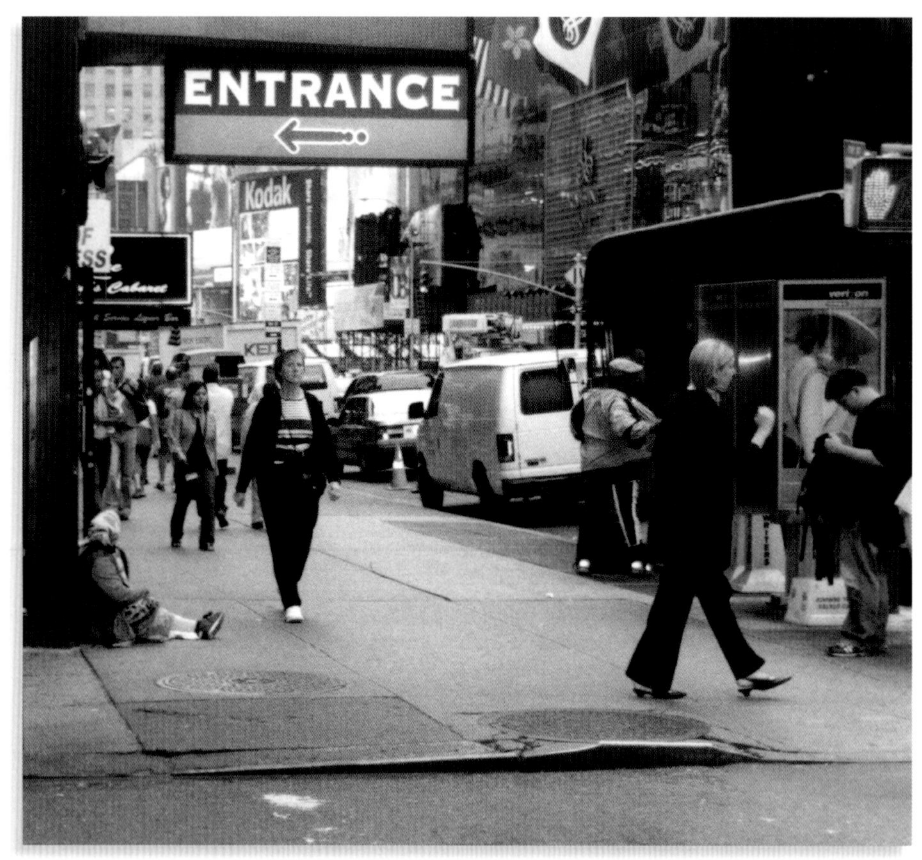

"What is the worst part about being homeless?" I asked.

"No one sees me."

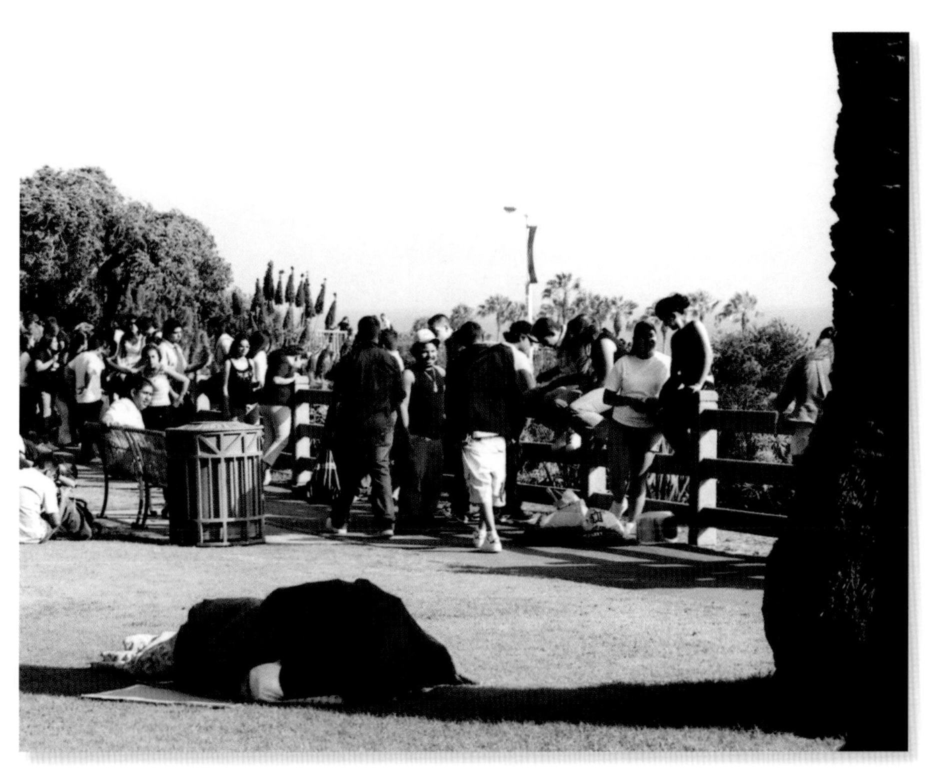

SANTA MONICA, CALIFORNIA

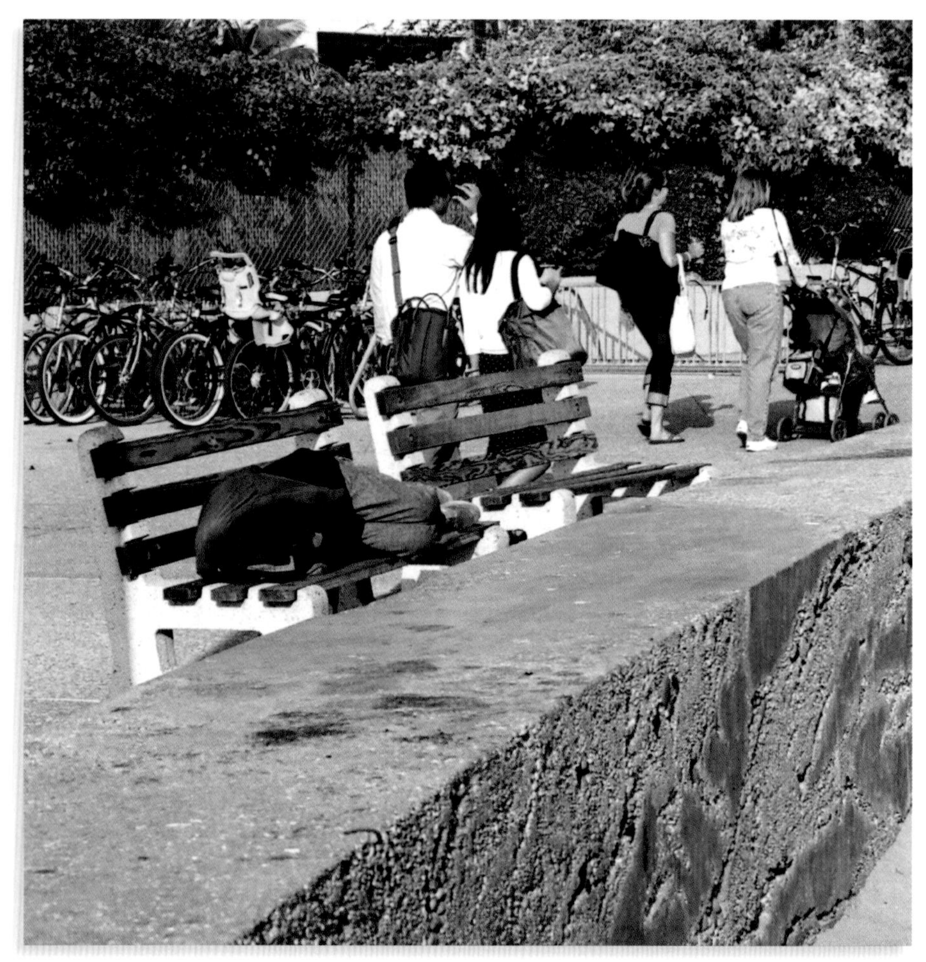

VENTURA BEACH, CALIFORNIA

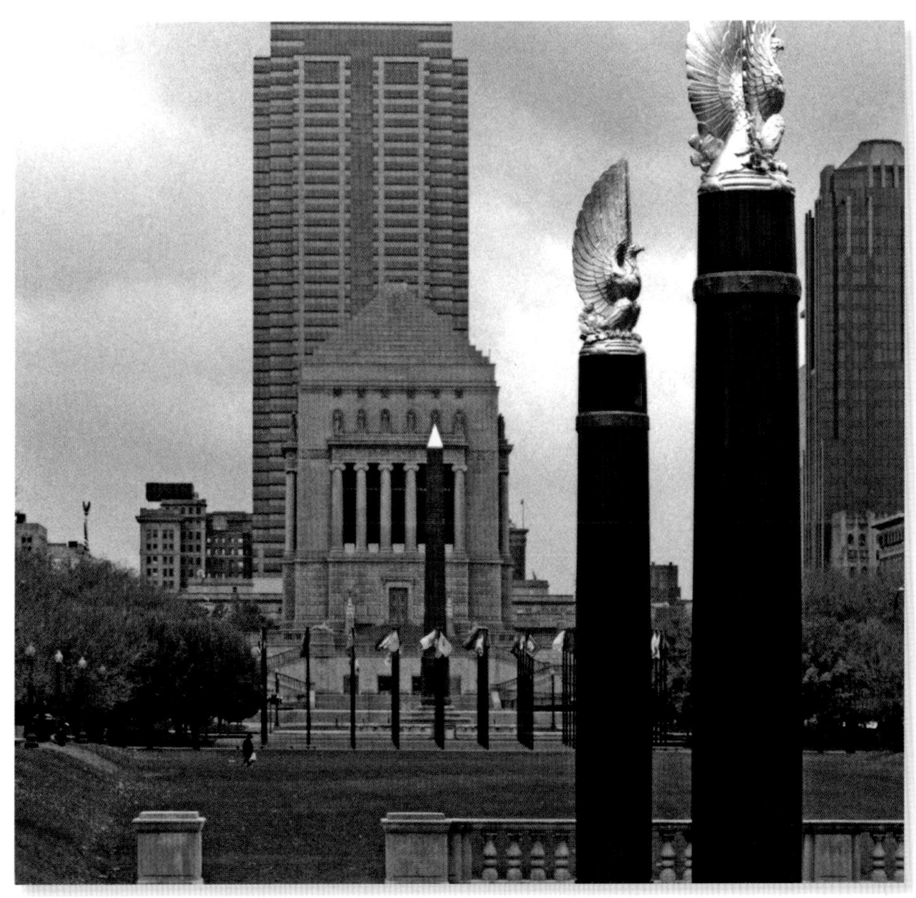

INDIANAPOLIS, INDIANA

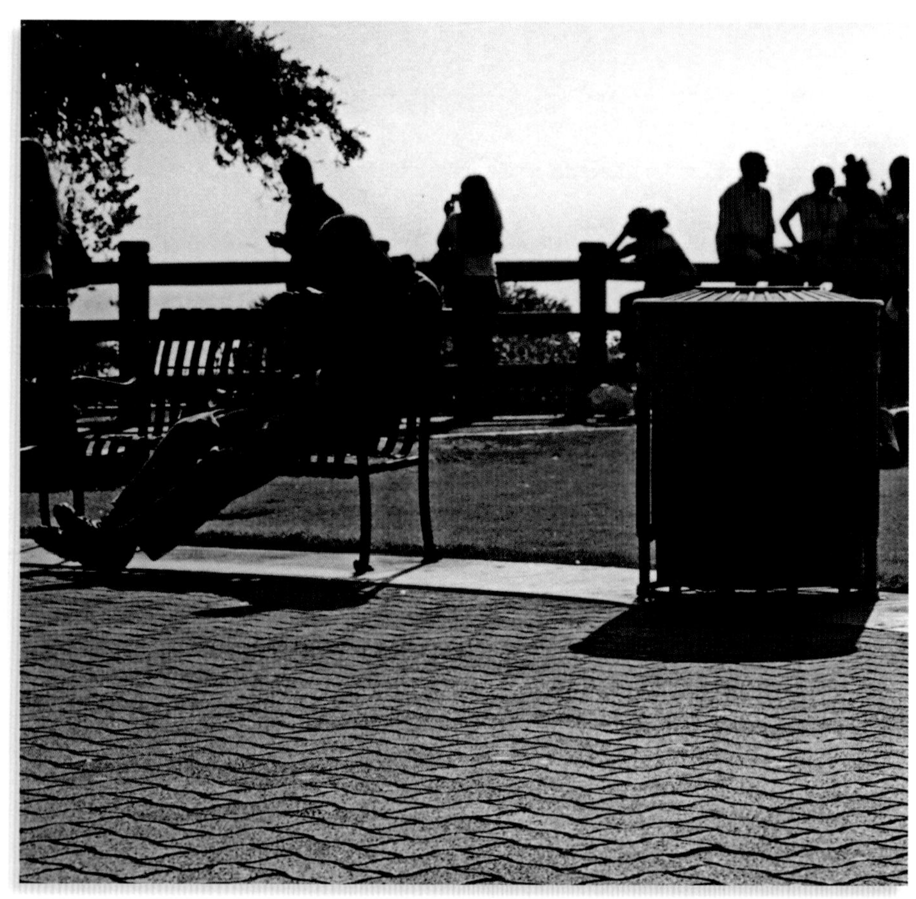

SANTA MONICA, CALIFORNIA

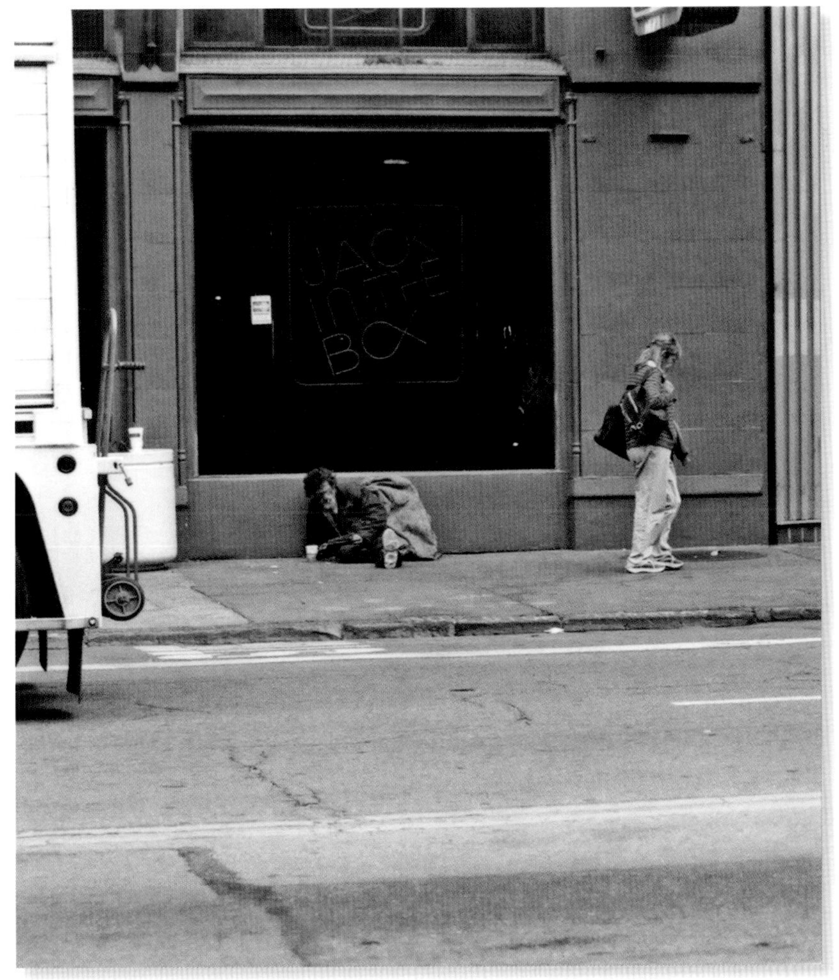

Sunday morning paper and a cup of coffee

San Francisco, California

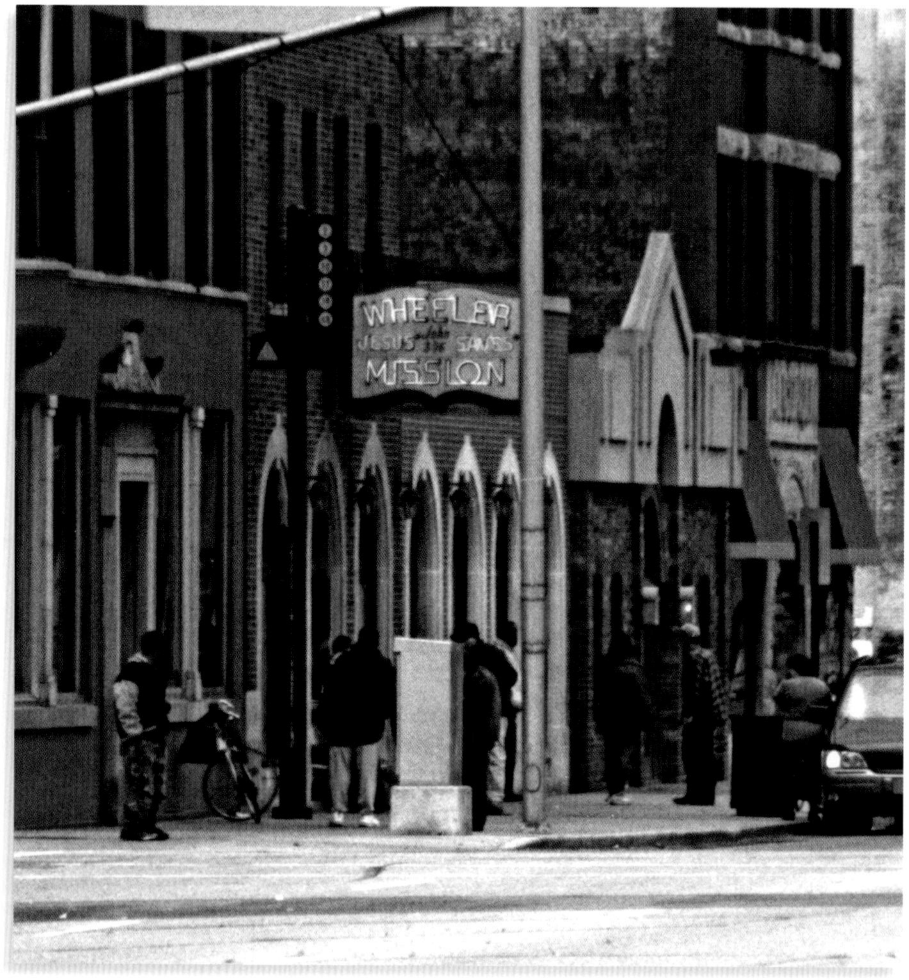

She was proud of the program she had established providing Sunday meals for the men from the shelter down the street.

He was impressed with what he saw and told her he could provide funds and volunteers from his church... they could create a partnership. He emailed her with the possibilities but there was never a response.

He was from a different denomination of the Christian faith. There would be no partnership.

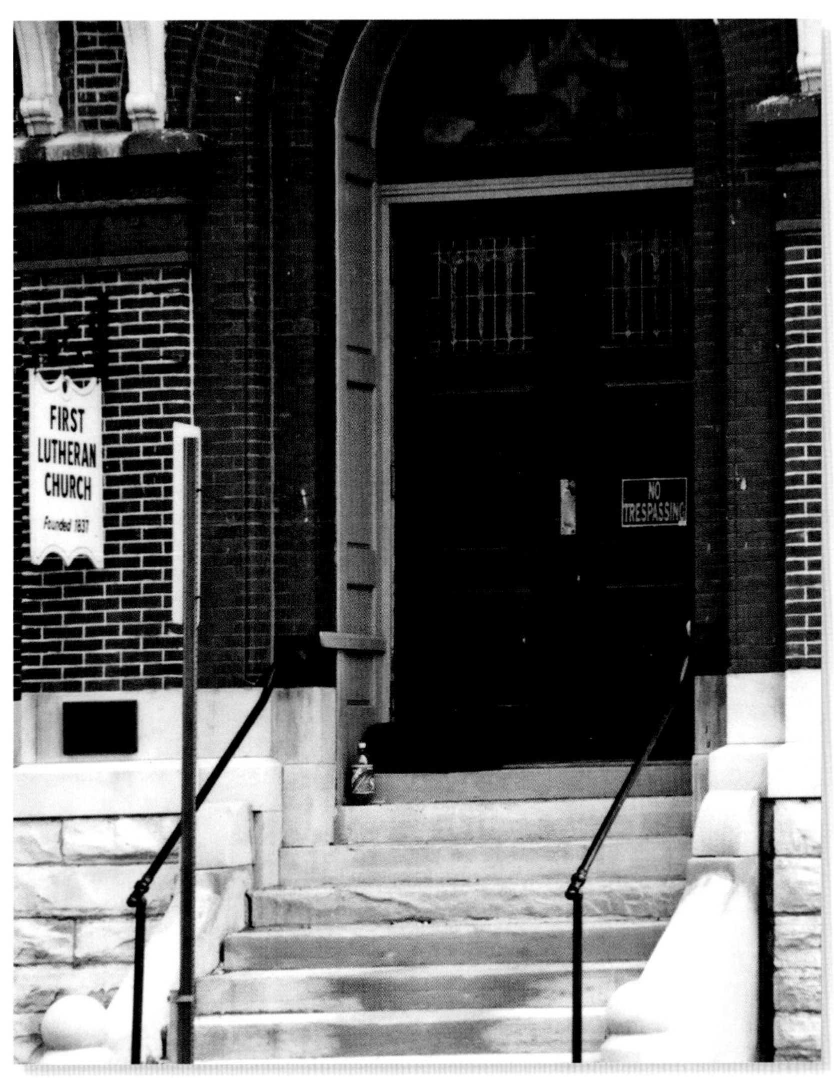

INDIANAPOLIS, INDIANA

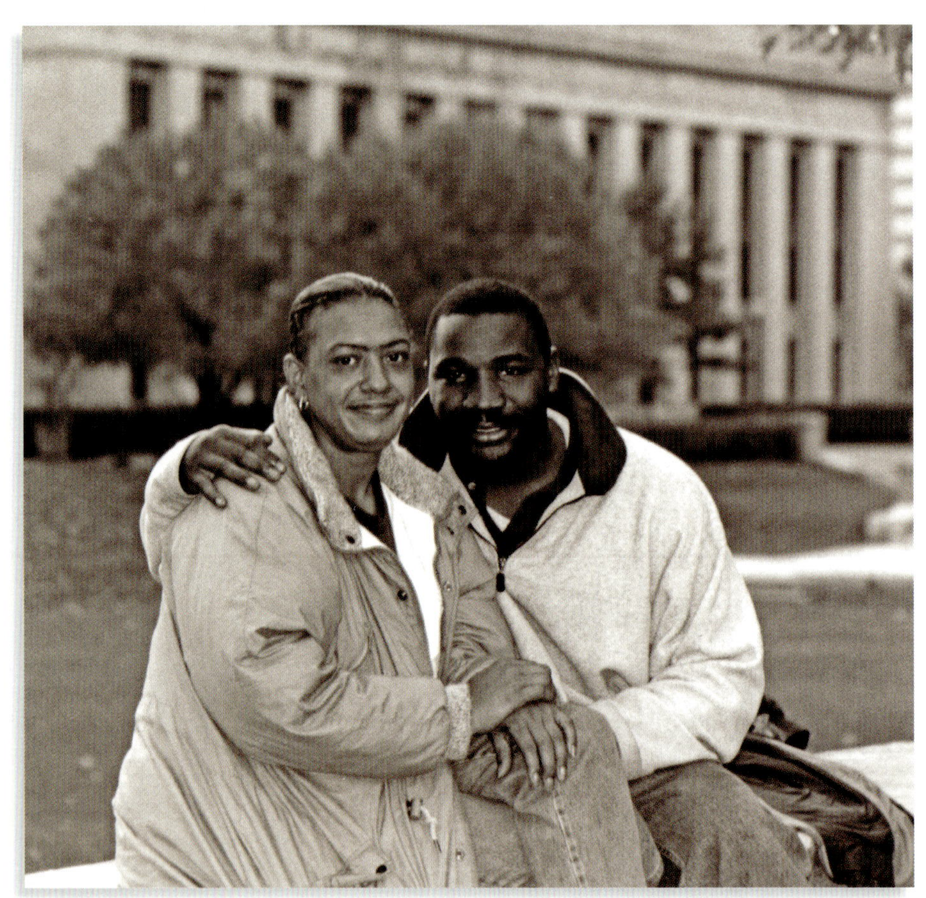

INDIANAPOLIS, INDIANA

I saw a couple on a park bench, he lying with his head on her lap. As I passed by, I could feel the love between them. He sat up and asked "Hey, can I have $85?" I stopped and laughed with him, a smile on both of our faces. "No, but if I can take your picture, I'll give you five."

We both got a deal. I admired the spunk. They had just lost their home. I hope he got a job as a salesman somewhere.

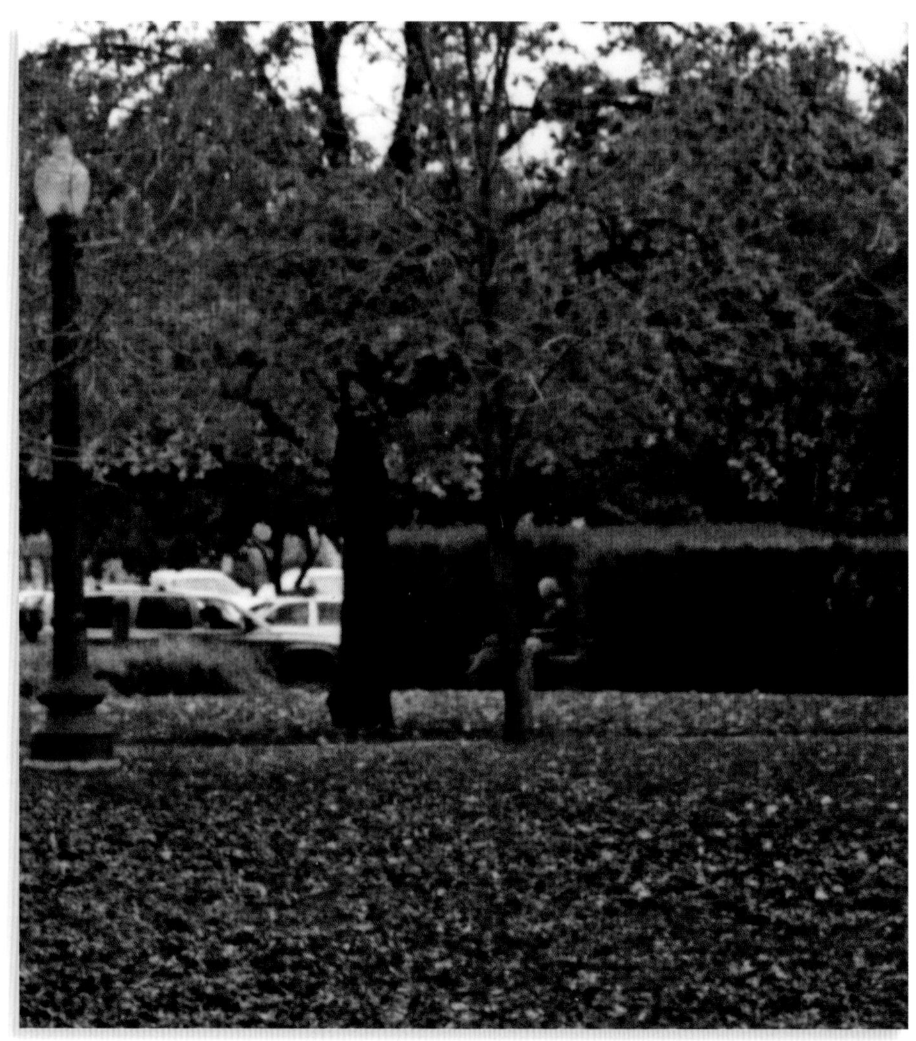

INDIANAPOLIS, INDIANA

"They kicked me out of the Army just because I hit my Master Sergeant. Dishonorable discharge. They wouldn't even give me my own gun back. They had to mail it back here to me. I spent six months in the brig. And he was wrong.

"And the guy I was working for here cheated everybody. We'd work ten hours and he'd pay us for eight. It's an auto body shop. Somebody's going to run him down in one of the cars they're working on. I called him on the hours we were paid for and he just fired me. Somebody's going to take him out.

"And now I'm here, no place to go with my family. Do you think my hair is bad? He said I should shape up, quit looking like I'm from the 'hood. He said I should show respect and act right. And then he fired me."

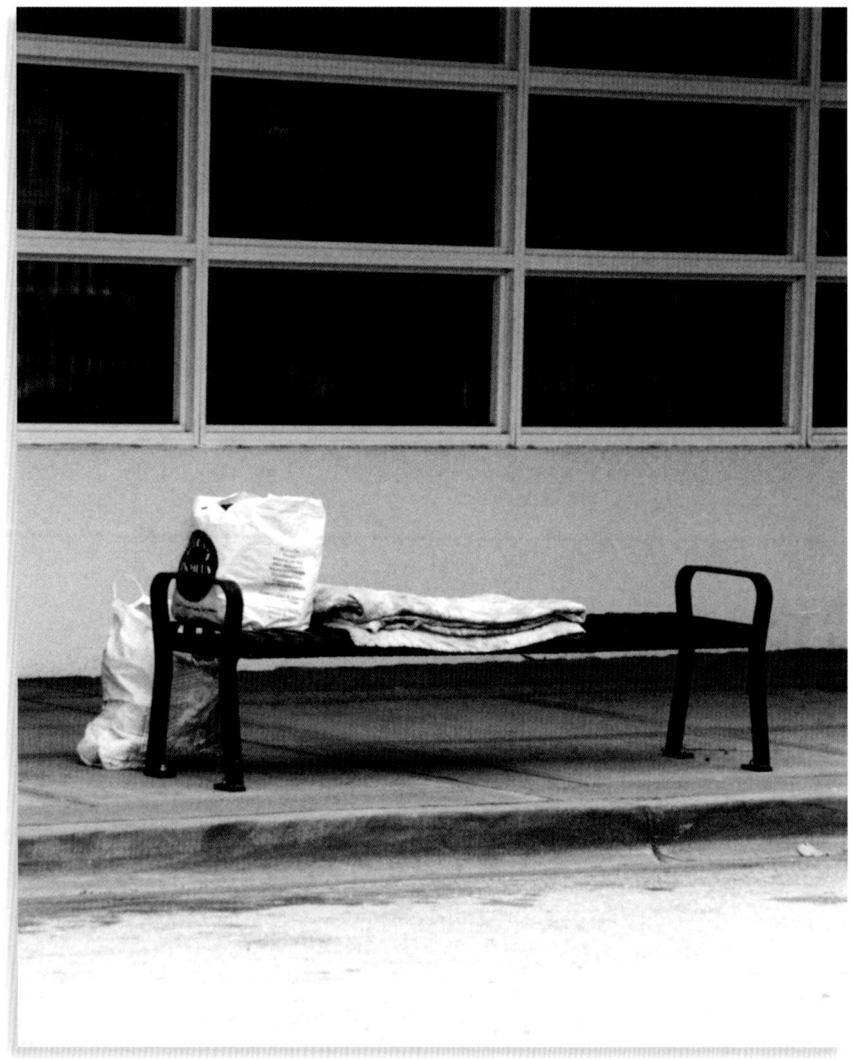

Where did Jesus live?

Where did Buddha live?

Where did Muhammad live?

PHOENIX, ARIZONA

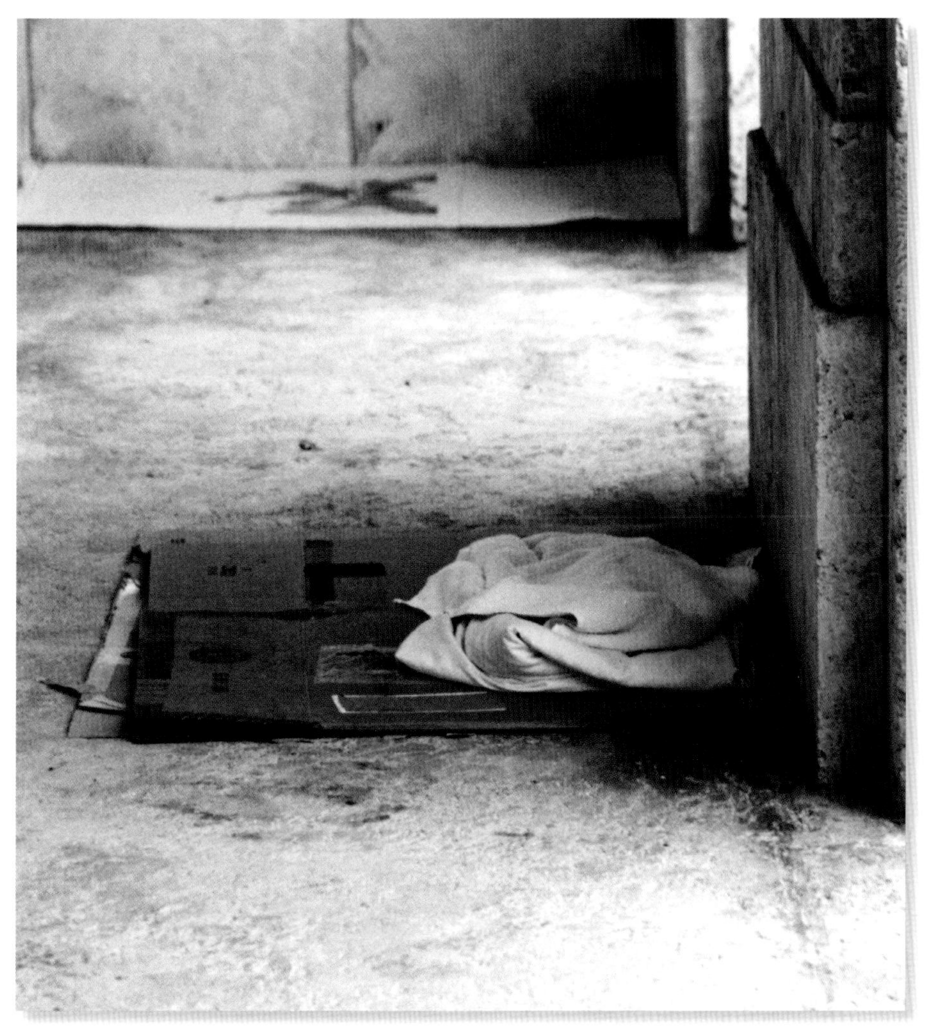

Where do you live?

PHOENIX, ARIZONA

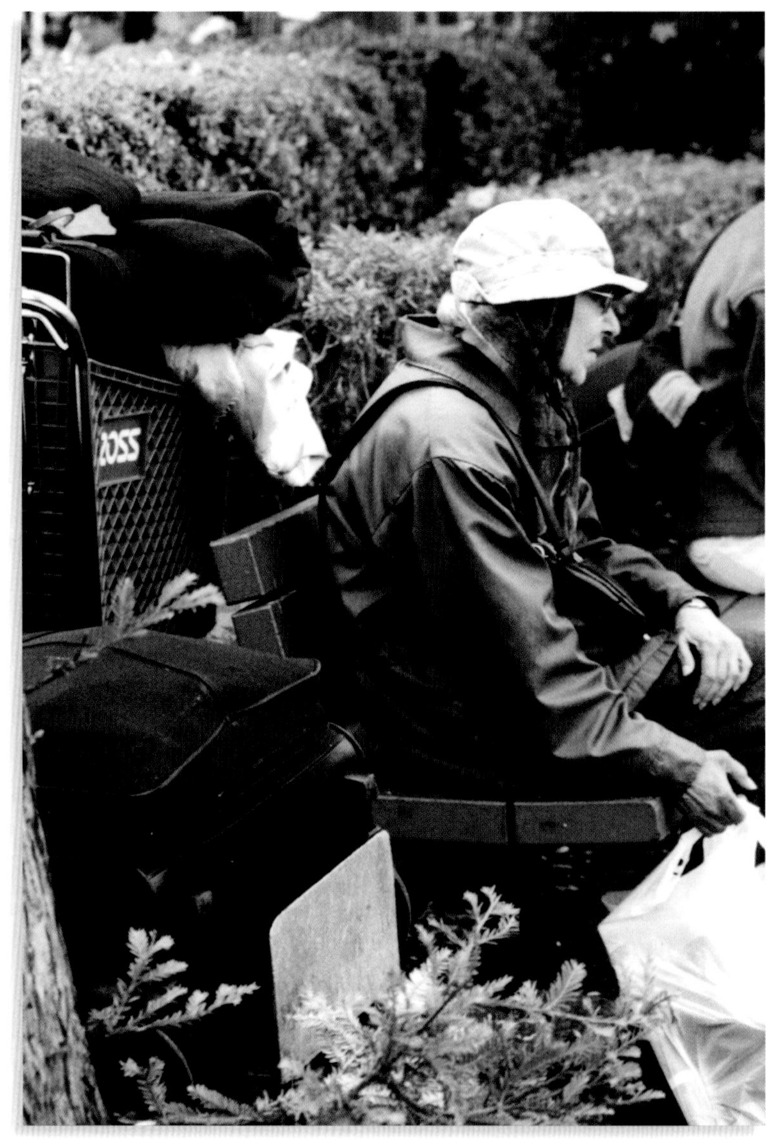

Whose mom is this?

She sat in a small park in front of a church, partially hidden by a tree; her belongings surrounded her. The Italian festival engulfed her with the aroma of food and the celebration of music.

Whose mom is this?

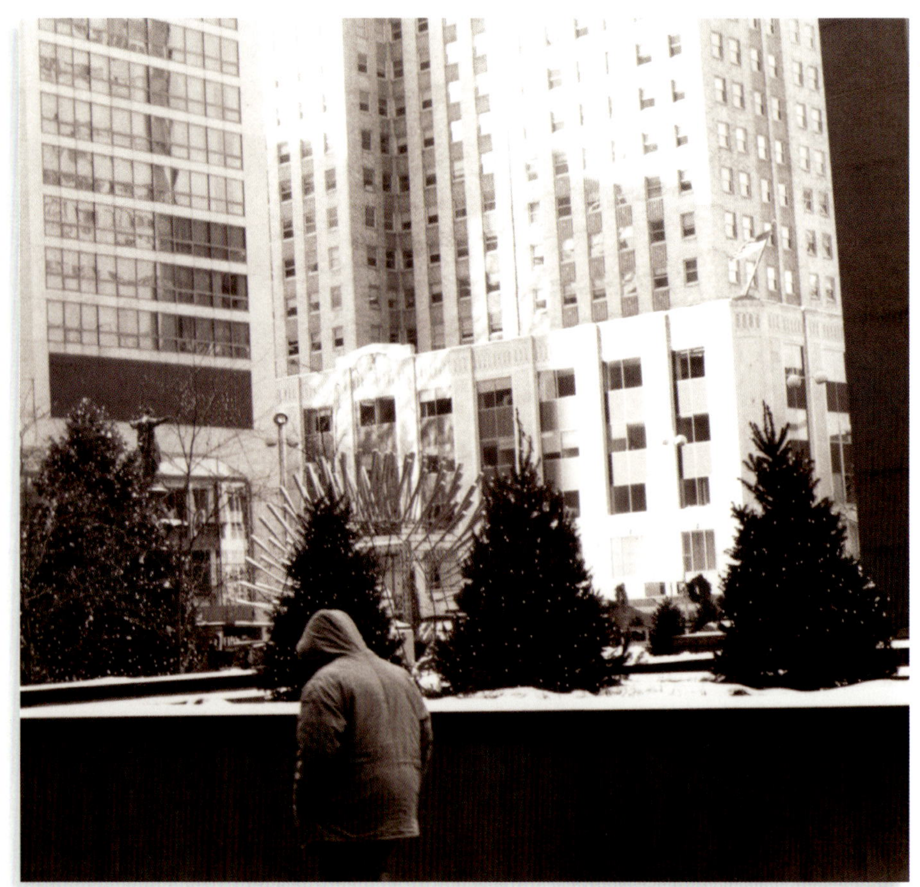

I am alone.

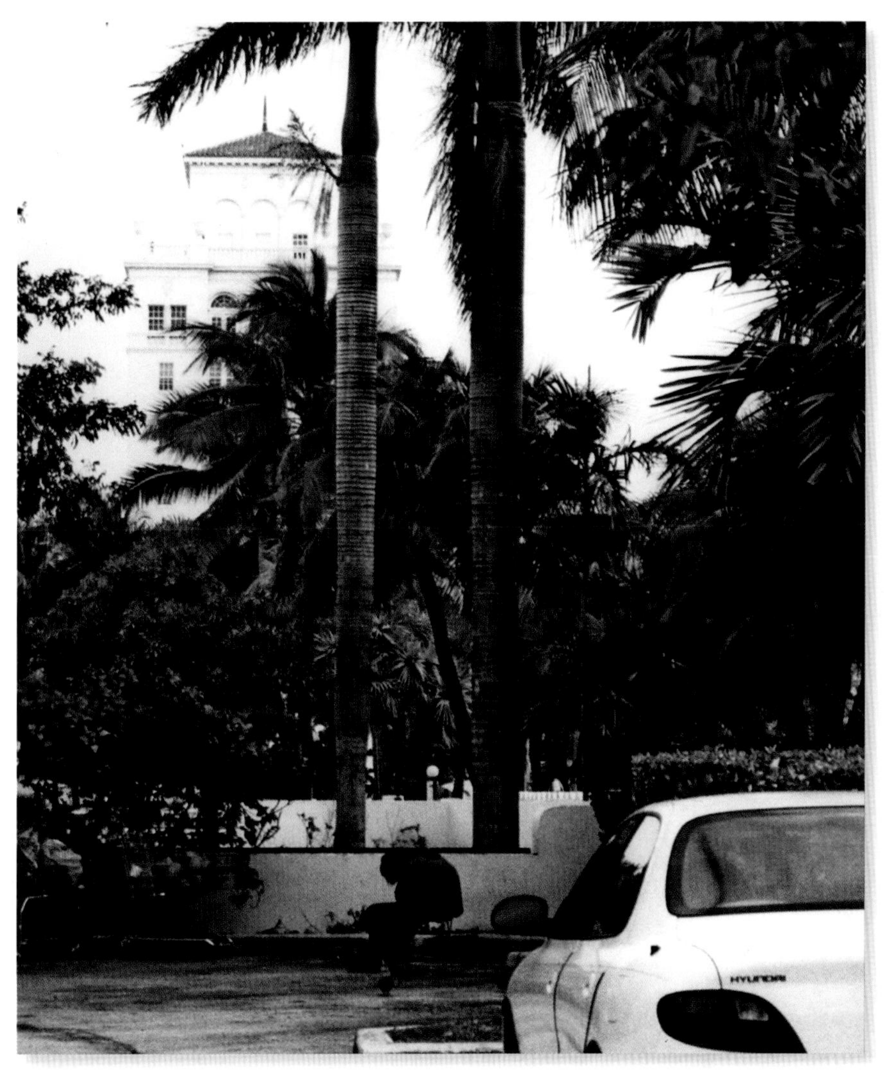

MIAMI, FLORIDA

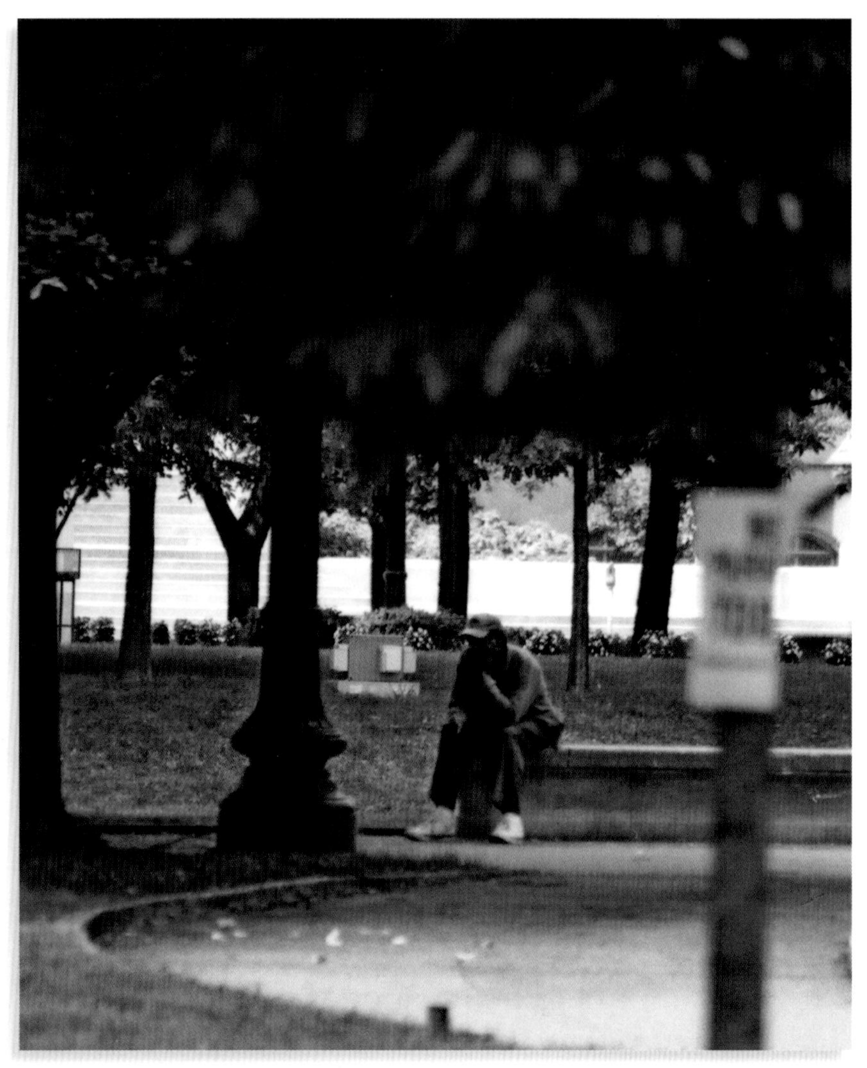

INDIANAPOLIS, INDIANA

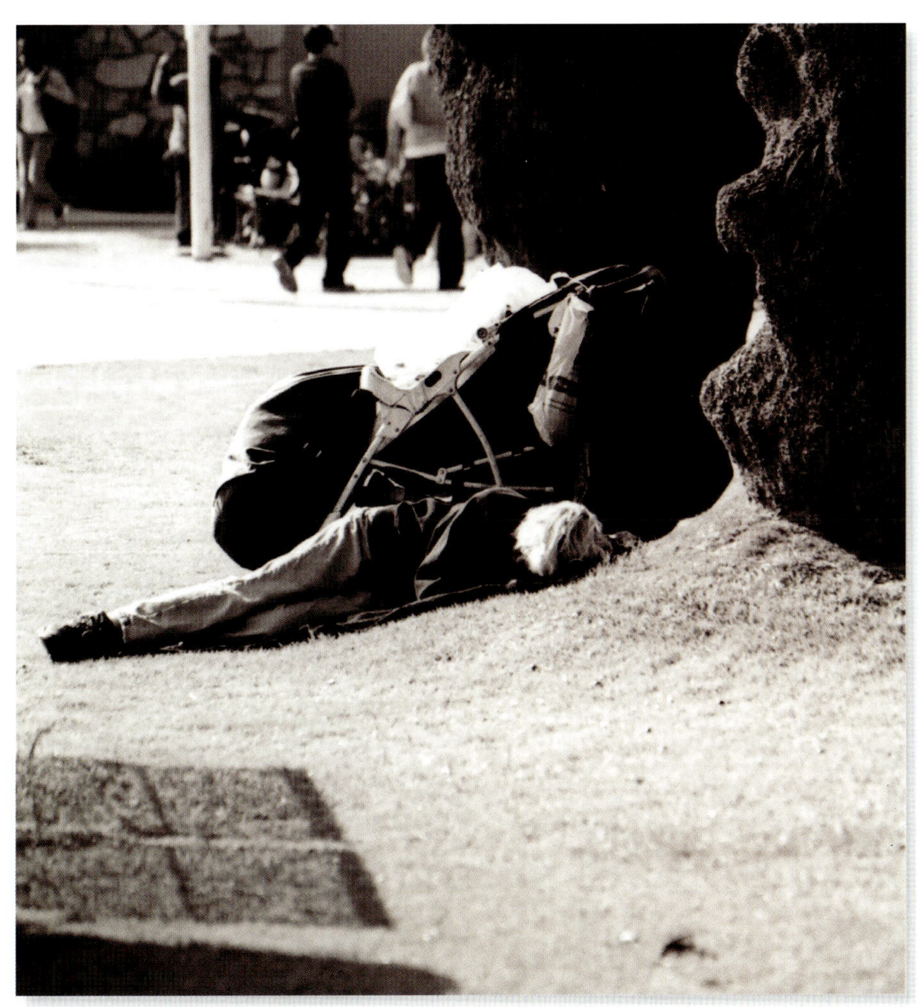

SANTA MONICA, CALIFORNIA

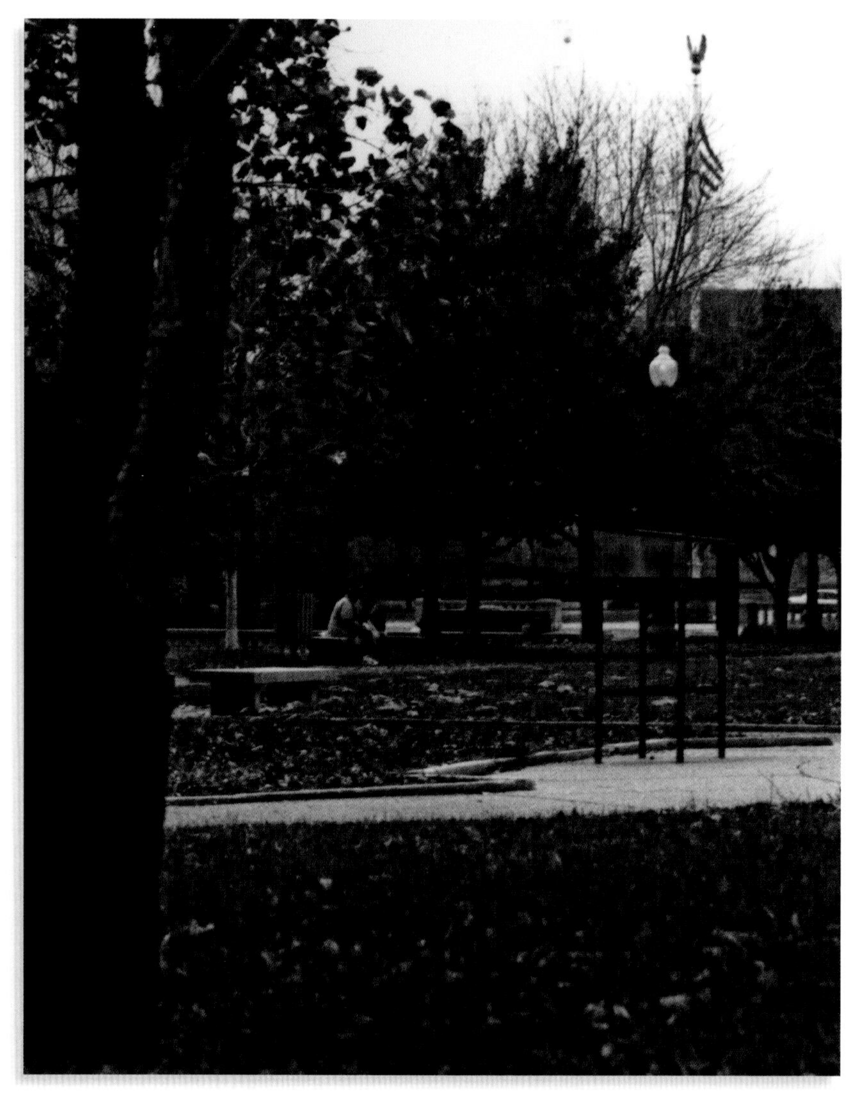

INDIANAPOLIS, INDIANA

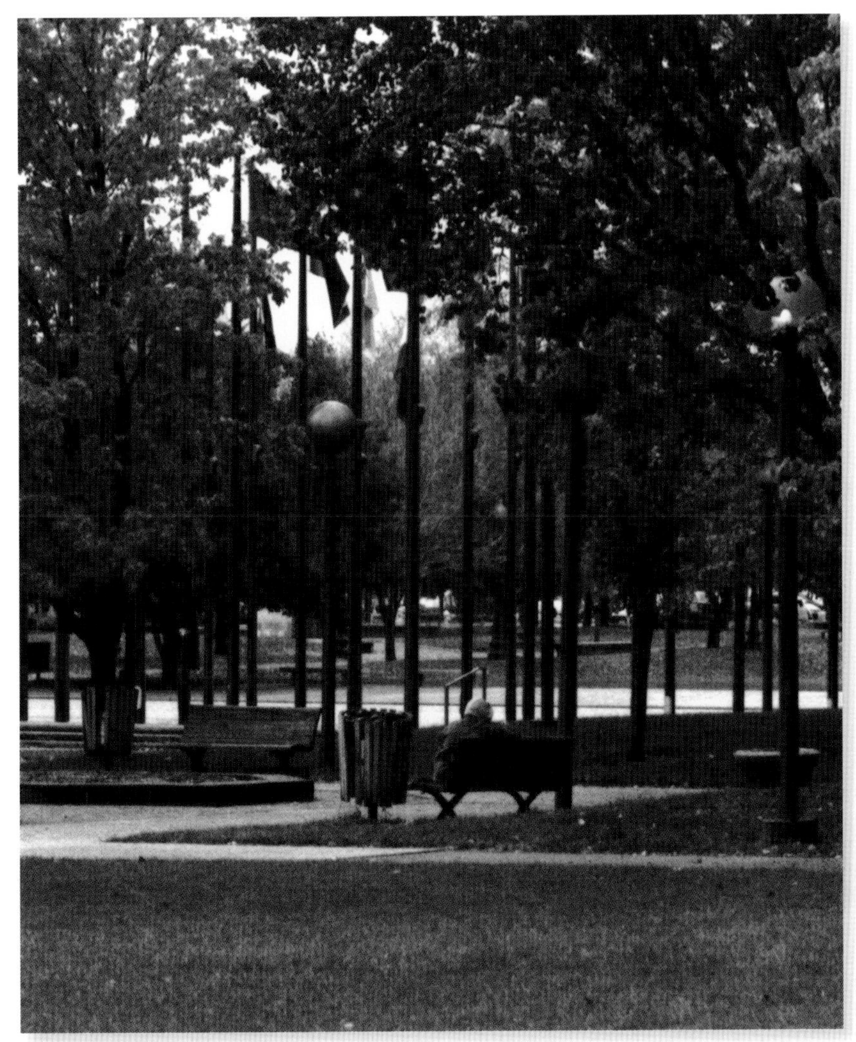

INDIANAPOLIS, INDIANA

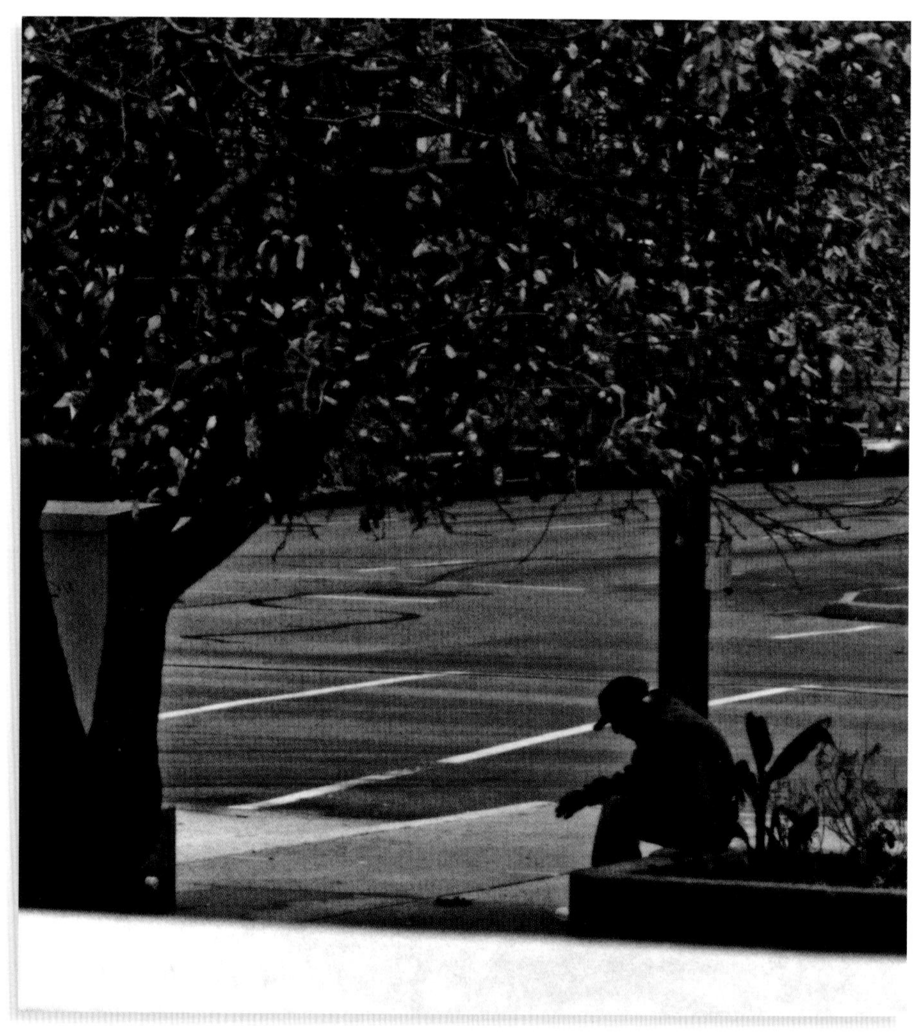

INDIANAPOLIS, INDIANA

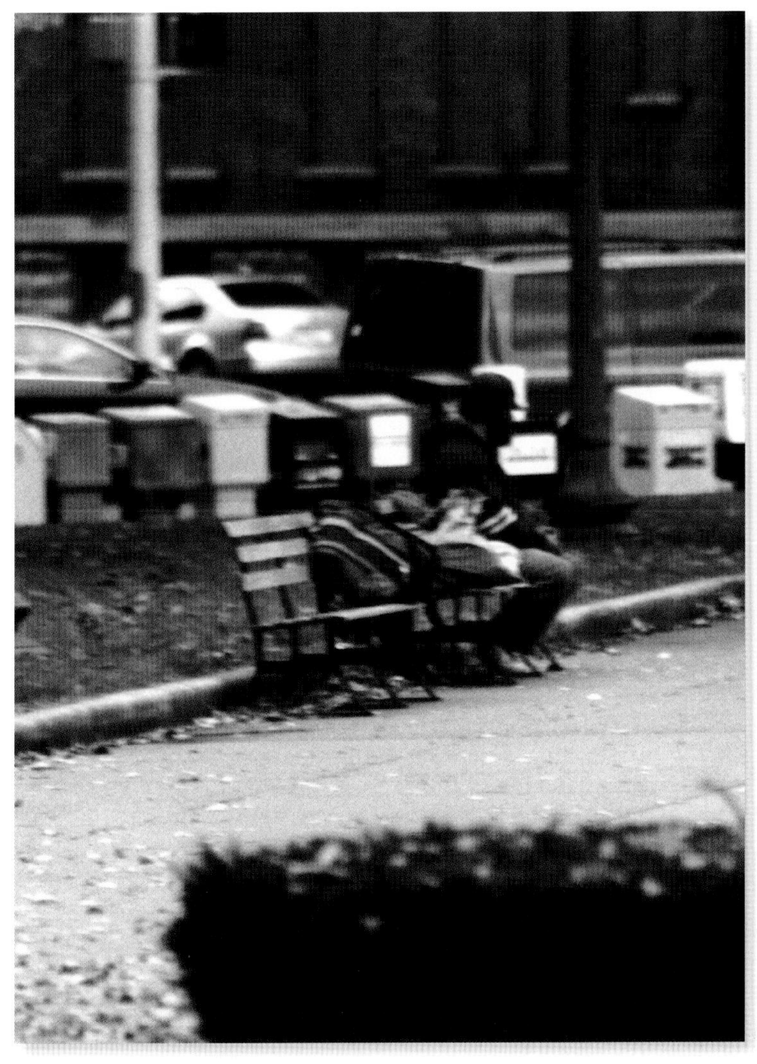

INDIANAPOLIS, INDIANA

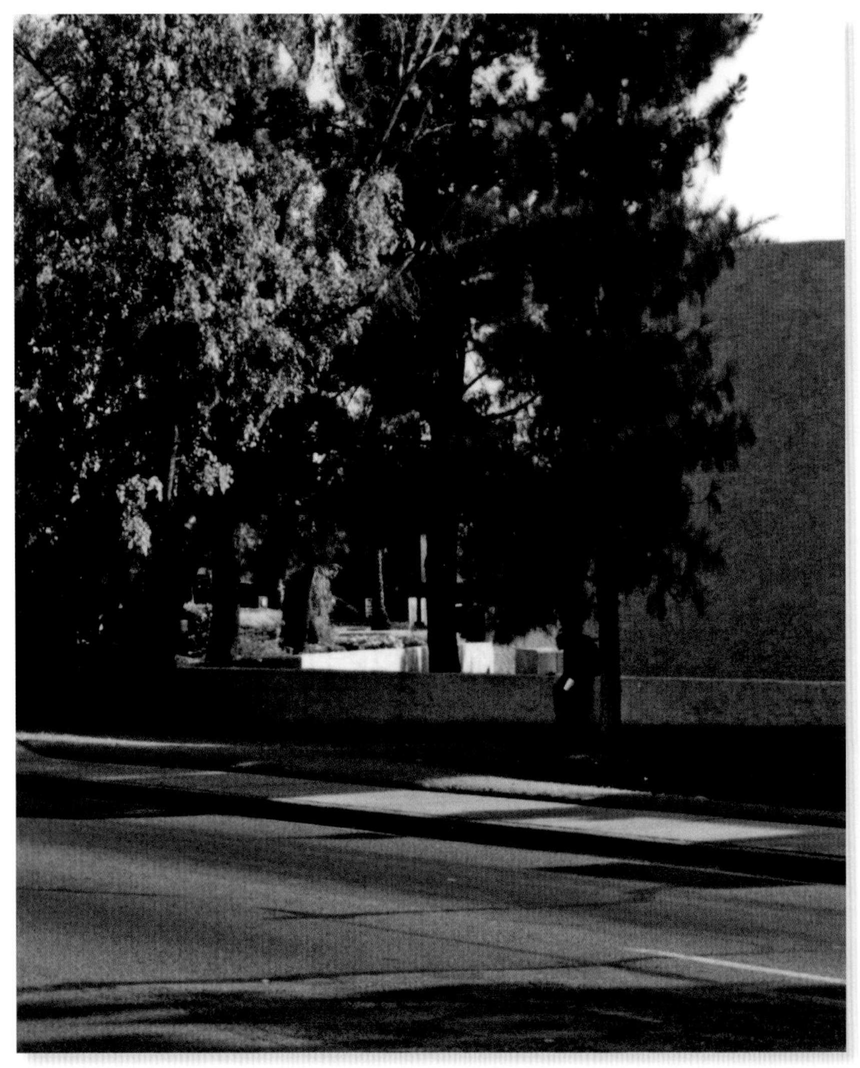

MESA, ARIZONA

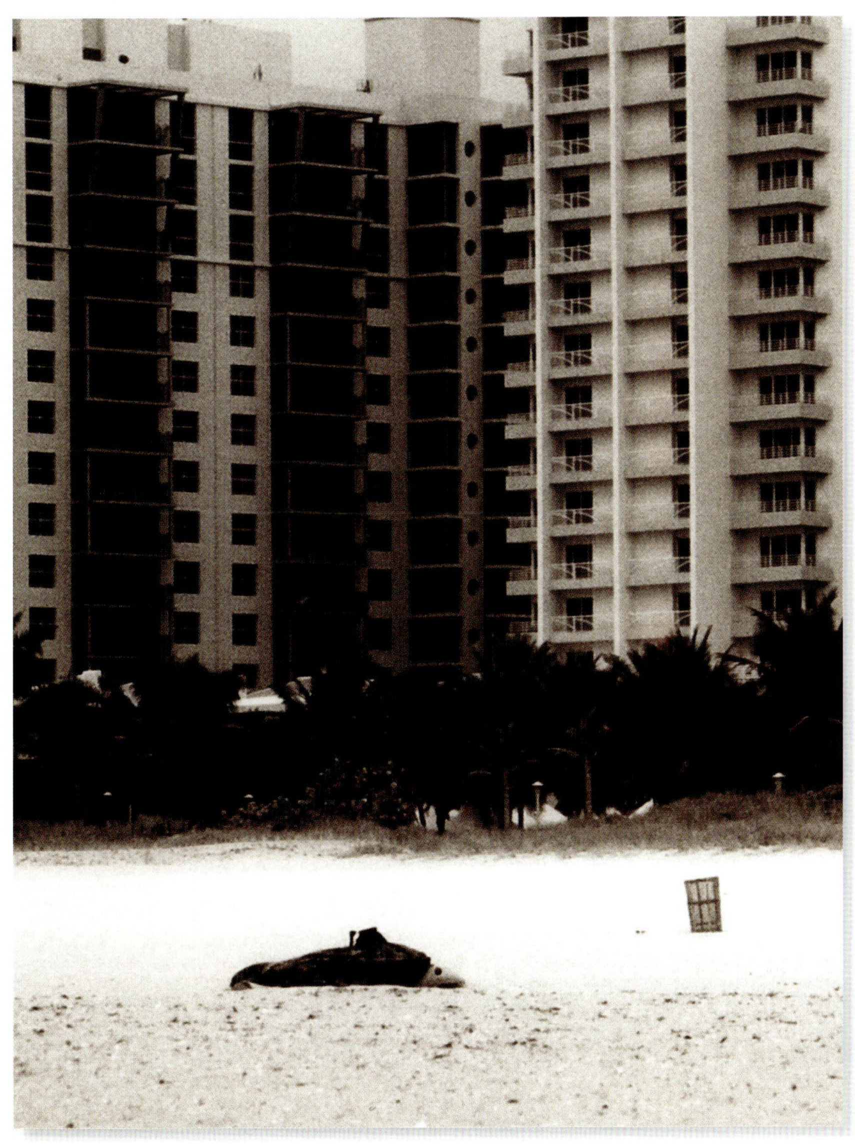

MIAMI, FLORIDA

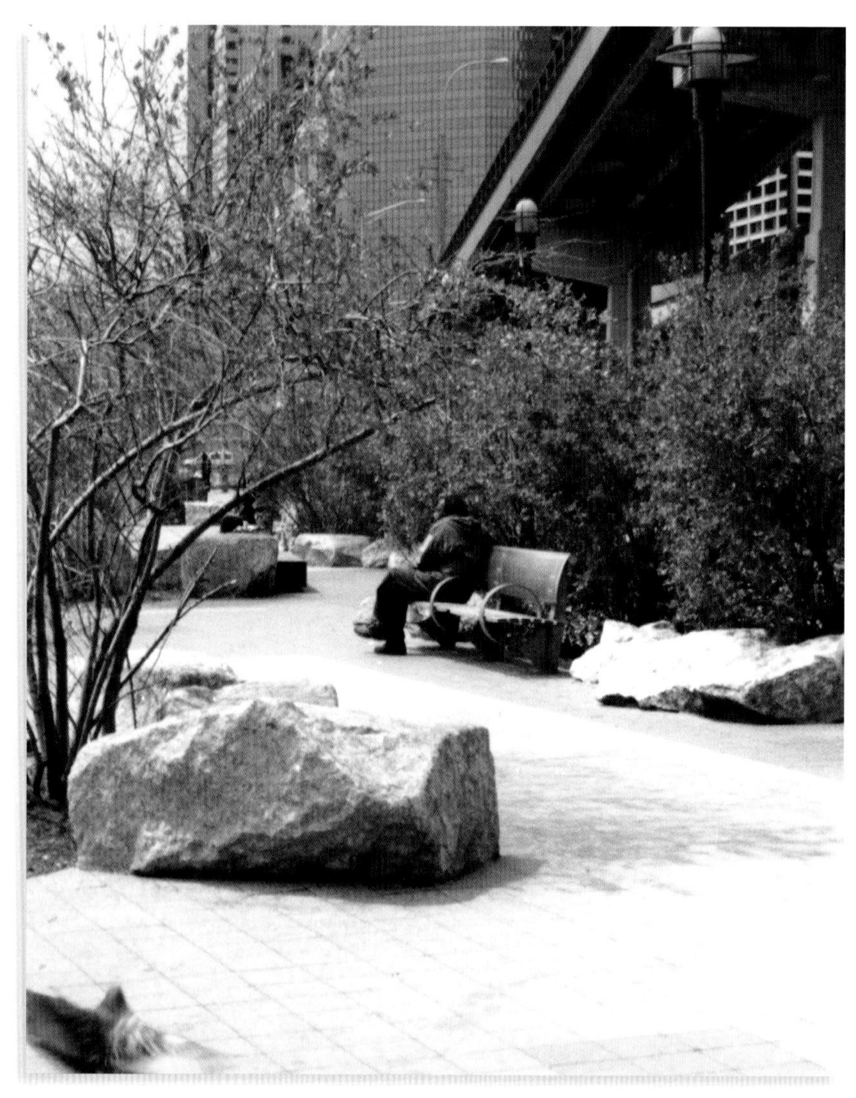

MANHATTAN, NEW YORK

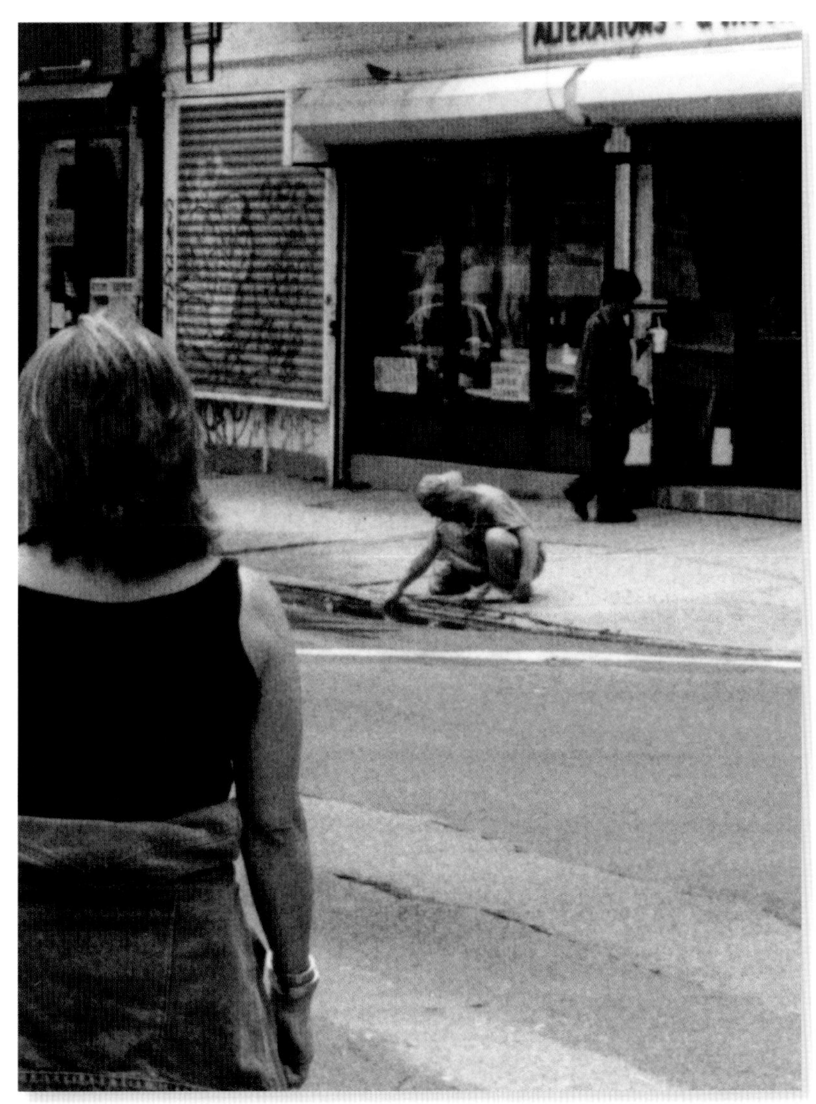

NEW YORK CITY, NEW YORK

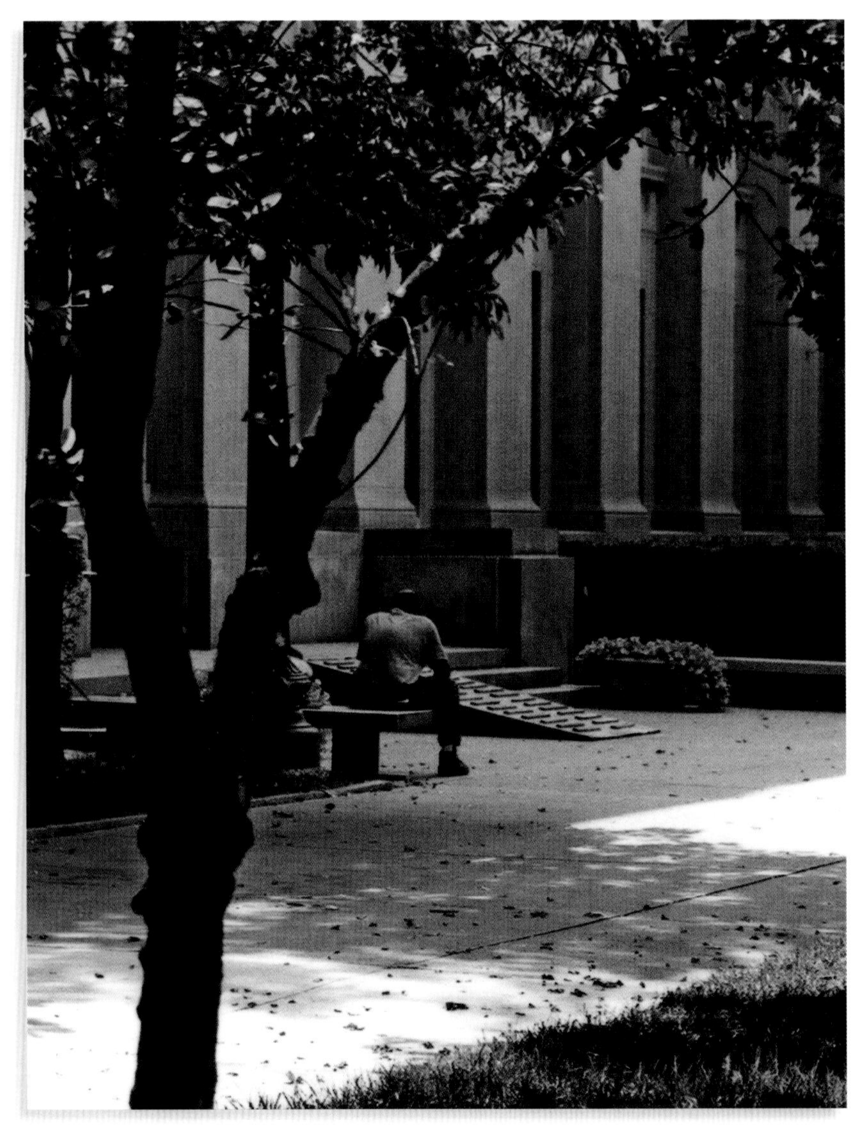

INDIANAPOLIS, INDIANA

I am alone on the streets of this city.

I am alone on the streets of this city and no one cares. No one is looking for me. No one knows who I am. No one knows who I was or where I came from.

I huddle in the doorways at night. I sleep under the bridge on rainy days. I sleep on the beach and in the park. I am alone.

I pick up your cigarette butts tossed on the street and I go through your trash thrown out. And I am alone.

I miss my home. I miss my parents and my brothers and sisters, my aunts and uncles.

God knows, I miss my children.

But I am alone.

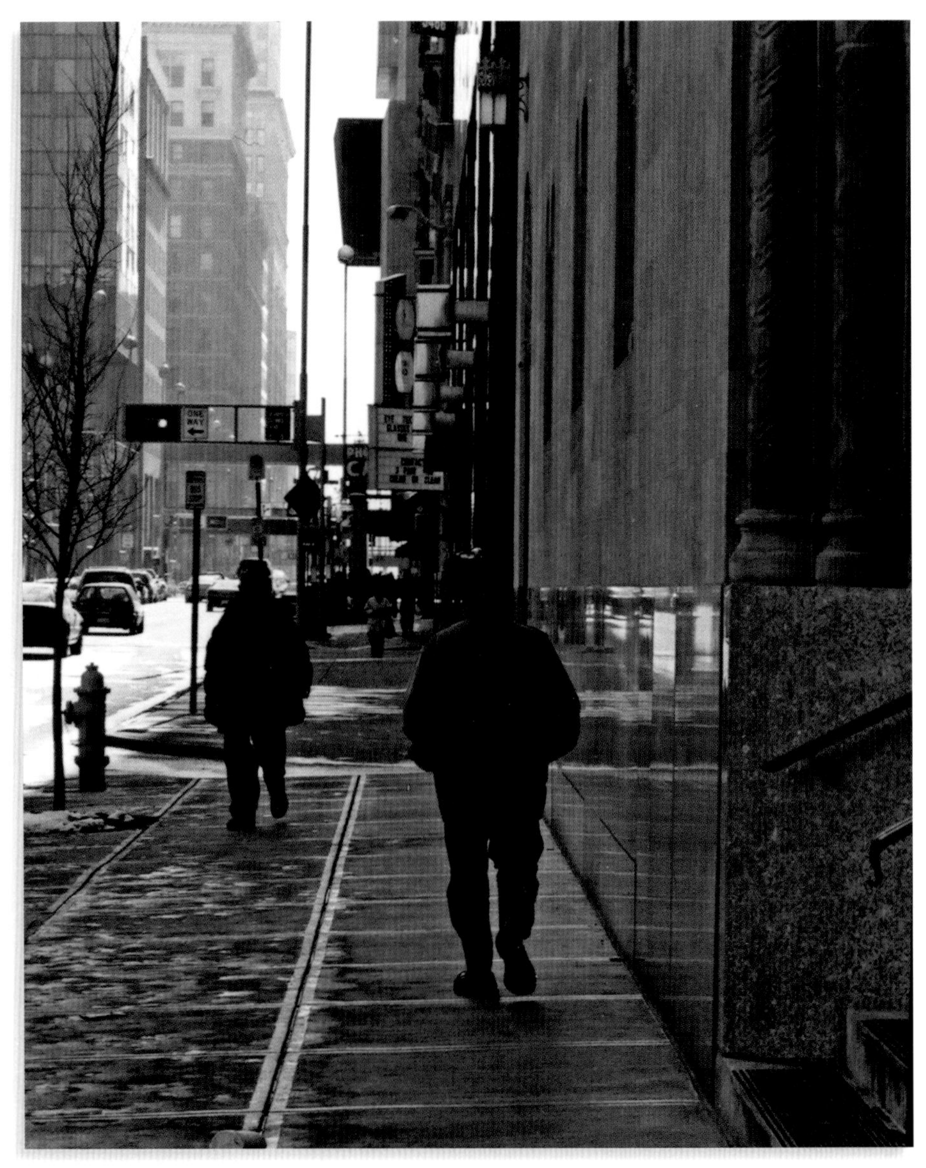

CINCINNATI, OHIO

I have discovered I have never stopped loving anyone I have ever truly loved. Relationships change, they go to the past, but the truest of love never ceases.

What happened to those who loved this man?

Did anyone love him? Where are they now?

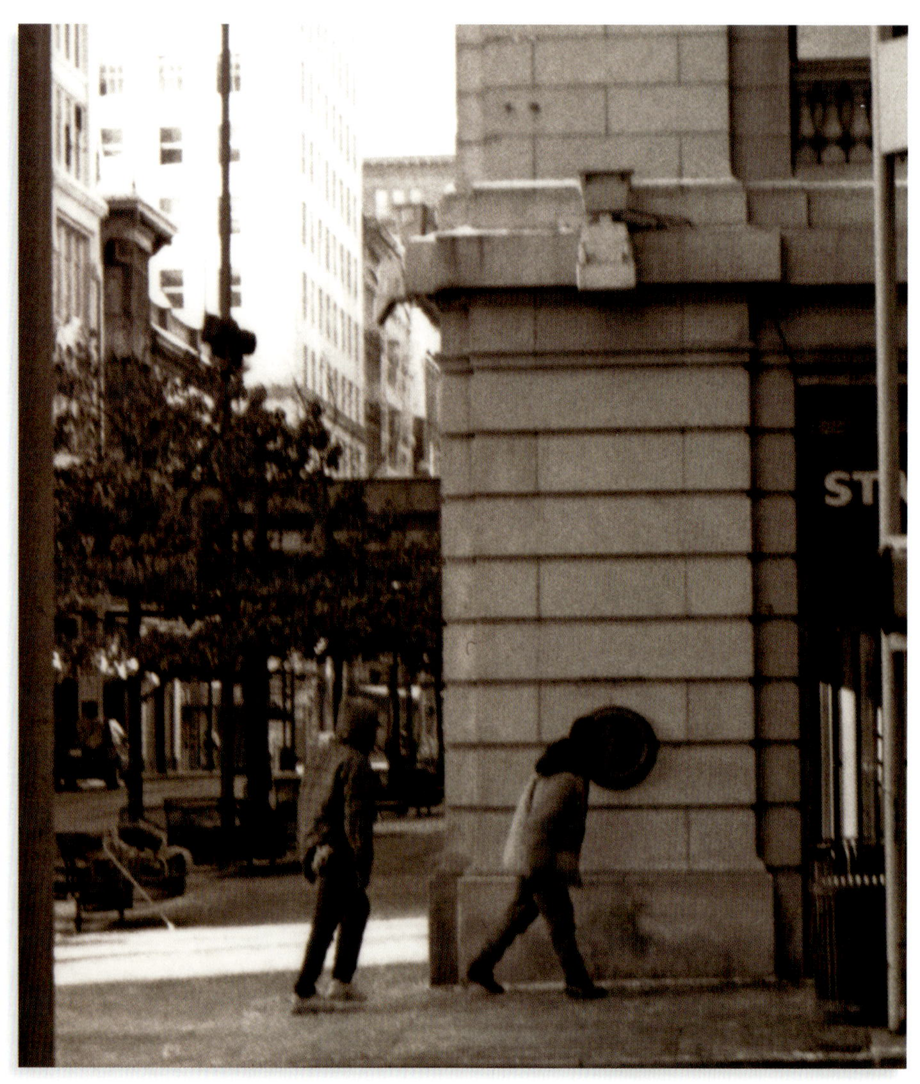

CINCINNATI, OHIO

It was the Saturday before Christmas and 18 degrees in downtown Cincinnati. At 9 a.m. there were a few people out, but the streets were cold and harsh.

While waiting for a crossing light to change, I heard a voice behind me wishing everyone he passed a Merry Christmas. He caught up to me and stood beside me. "I hope you and your family have a very Merry Christmas," he said. The smile was toothless. The face had been unshaven for days. He bounced off the curb when the light changed and strode ahead, his shoes holey and without socks. Yet he had given me a gift... his best wishes.

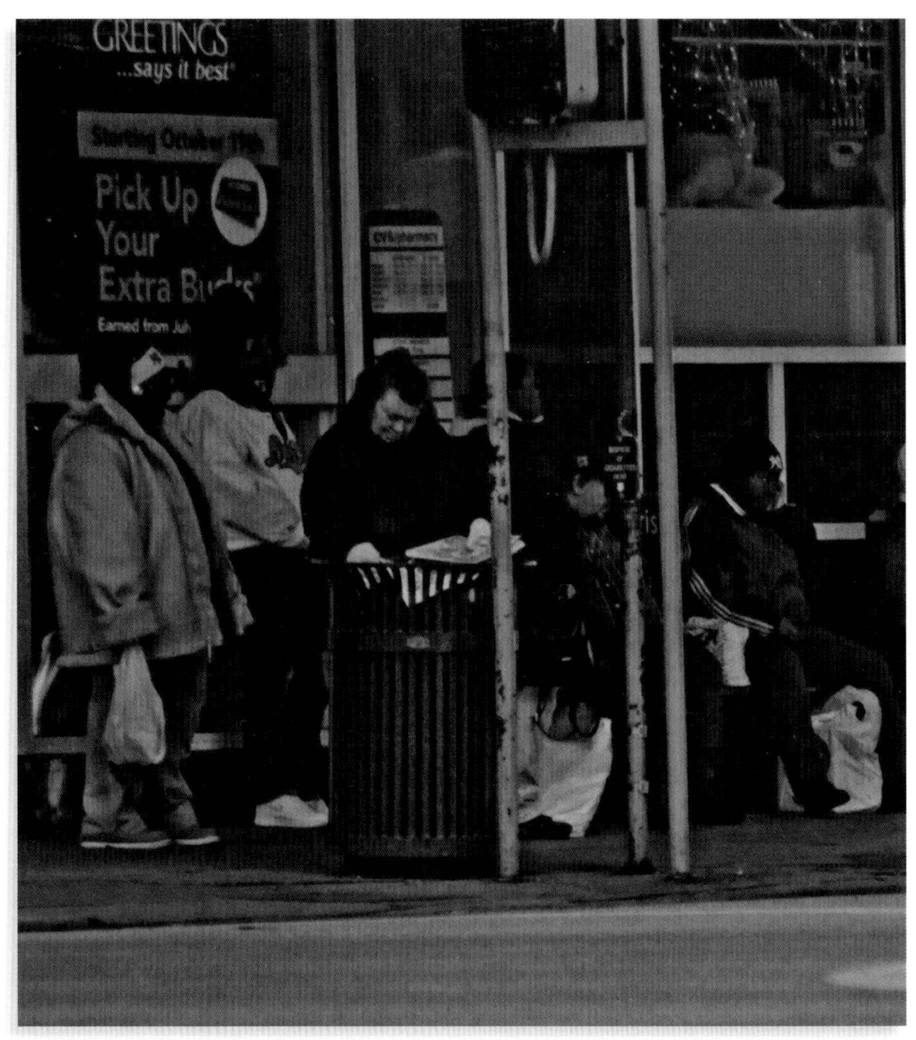

CINCINNATI, OHIO

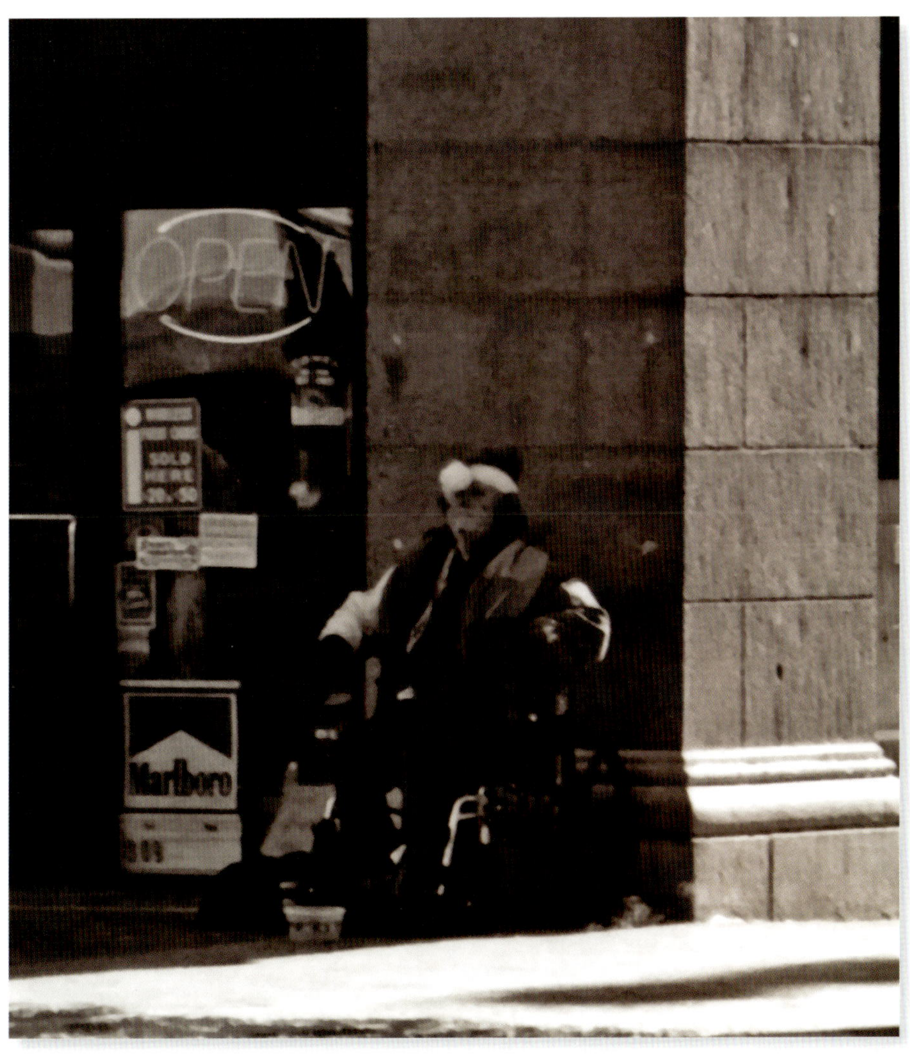

CINCINNATI, OHIO

A conversation with Demetrius

"Hey, Dave, let's go smoke." We stopped outside the office and I handed him a cigarette. I had known Demetrius for close to ten years and this was as bad as I had ever seen him. It was an early March day.

He cocked his head to the left, as he often did when he talked. "The last few months have been bad, Dave, really bad."

"Where were you living before you started staying under the bridge, Demetrius?"

"I was with my niece, but she let her man move in and I had to leave." He had lost a couple more teeth and his bicycle since the last time I saw him. His hair was matted and his clothes were dirty.

"Sometimes I stay with my woman friend but I can't do that all the time because she has other men friends."

"What are you doing for work?"

He replied that he was doing odd jobs and construction labor, but there wasn't much work now. "The past months have been hard, Dave," he repeated.

"Why don't you try one of the shelters?"

"Too many mens, man, too many mens. You know what I mean?"

A friend of mine had recognized him sitting on the sidewalk downtown with a cup, silently begging, not far from the railroad bridge under which he was living—the same railroad bridge where Not Willie, the man who prayed for me, had been living three years prior.

"Are you doing drugs, Demetrius?"

"Naw, man, you gotta have money to do that, Dave." The head cocked again.

My friend had given him enough money for dinner the night before and the bus fare from downtown to the west side where he could do some odd jobs and earn some money.

We smoked another cigarette. He had come early to work. But he and I both knew that his coming early wouldn't last.

"What are you going to do with the money you earn today, Demetrius?"

"I'm going to get a warm room tonight and get cleaned up. I'm going to wash my clothes and eat. And I'm going to try to see my little girl. Maybe tomorrow I can find some work."

Take care, Demetrius.

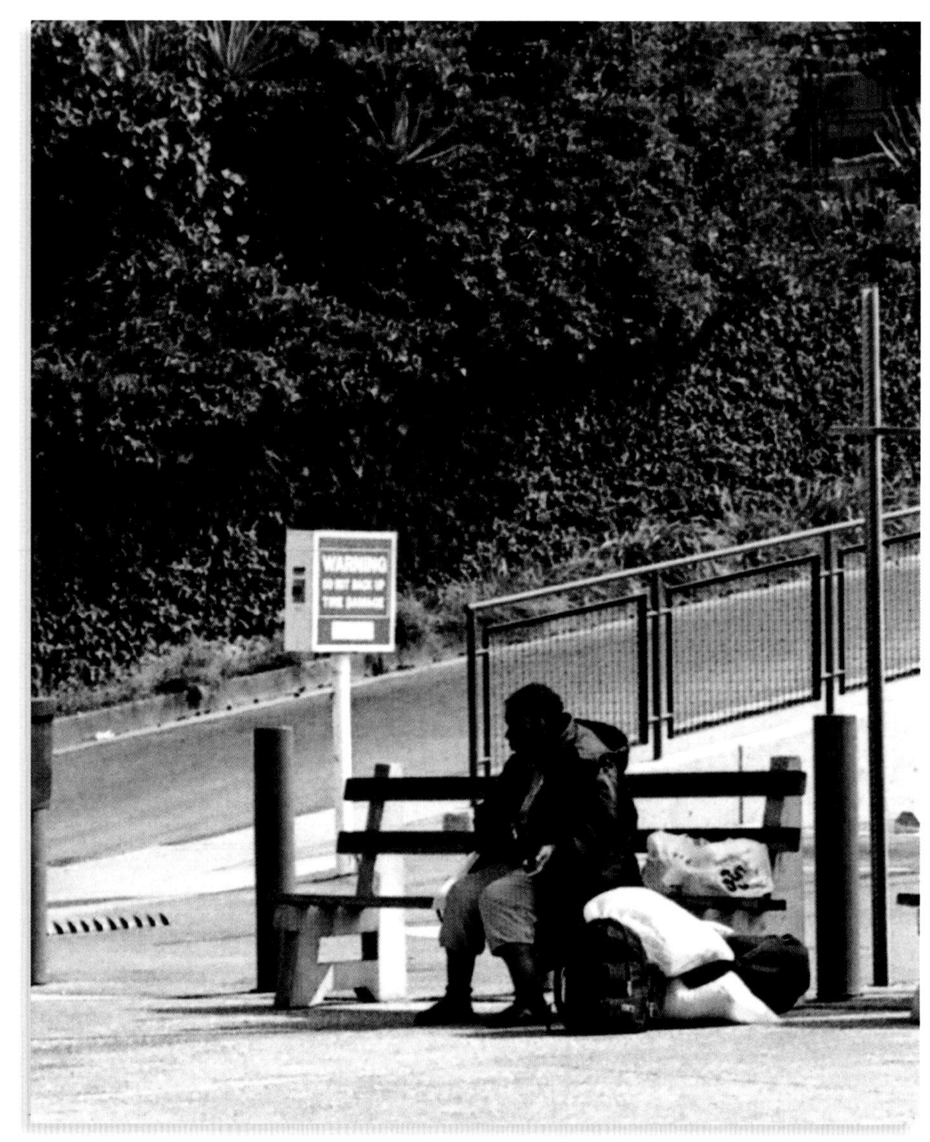

SANTA MONICA, CALIFORNIA

Patti on the plane.

"Santa Monica is a mecca for the homeless. The city is very open for them. Remember, there are three kinds of them: the alcoholics and those with addictions, the mentally ill, and those who choose that life."

This is obviously an oversimplification; there are many reasons for homelessness.

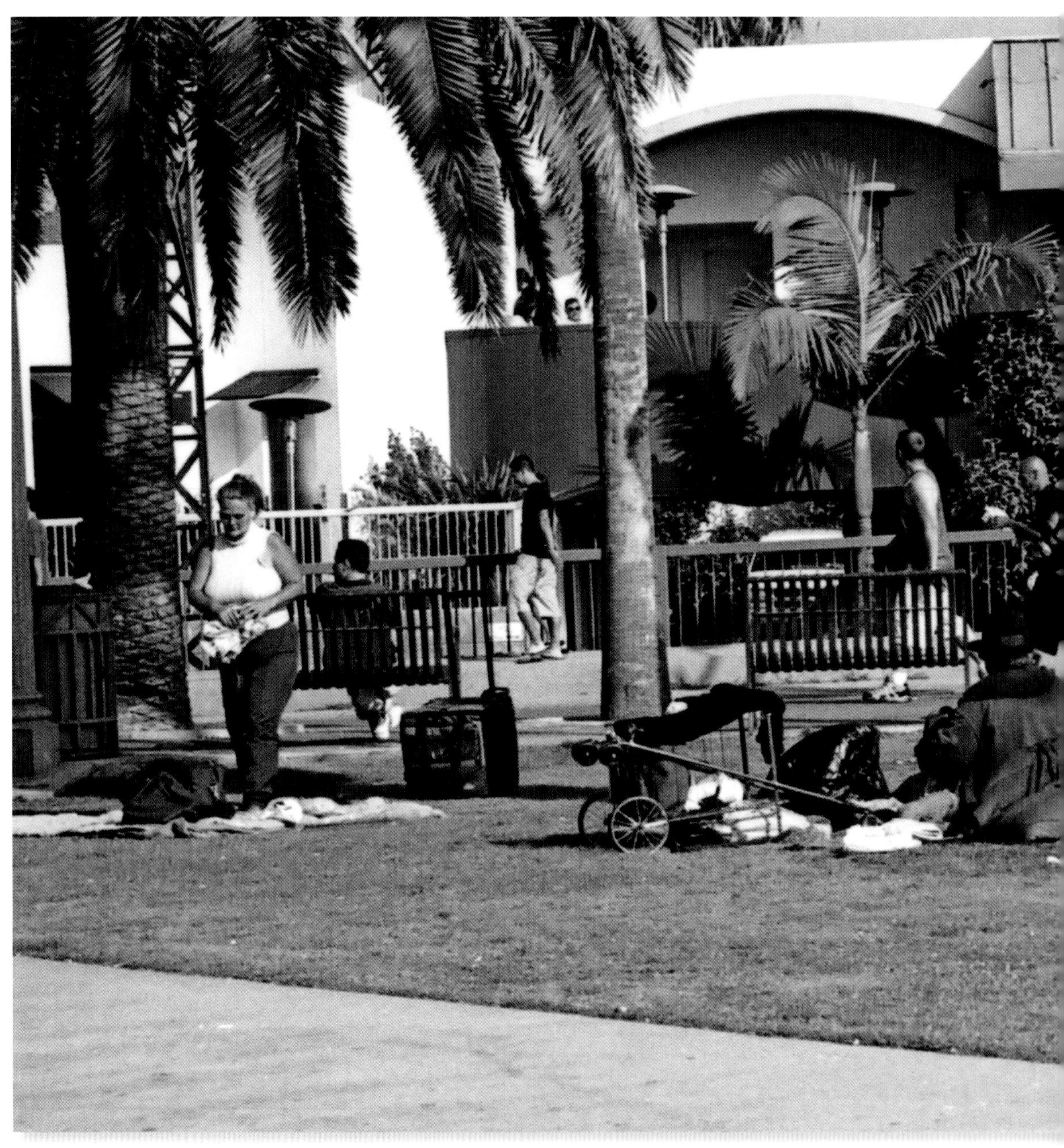

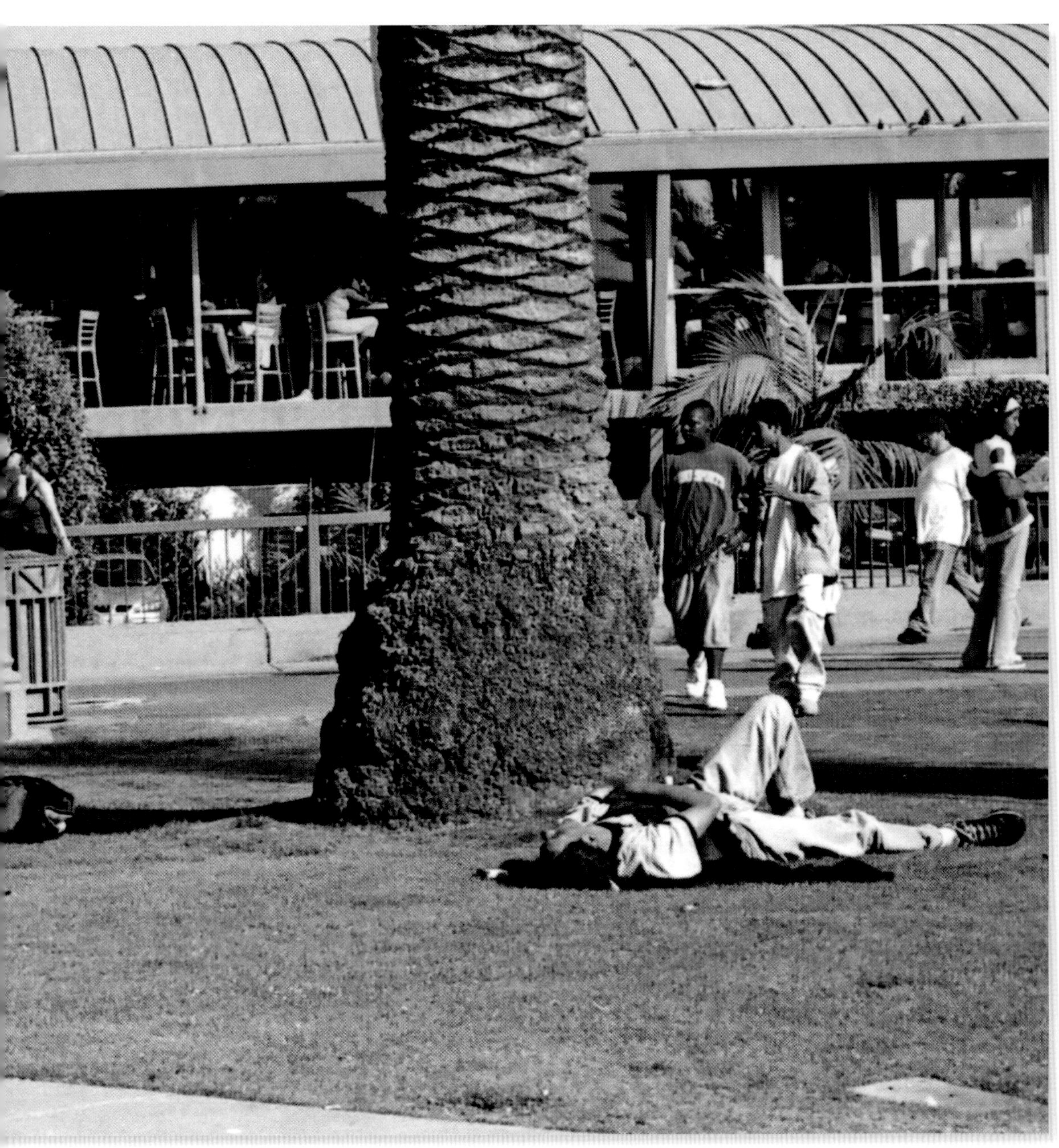

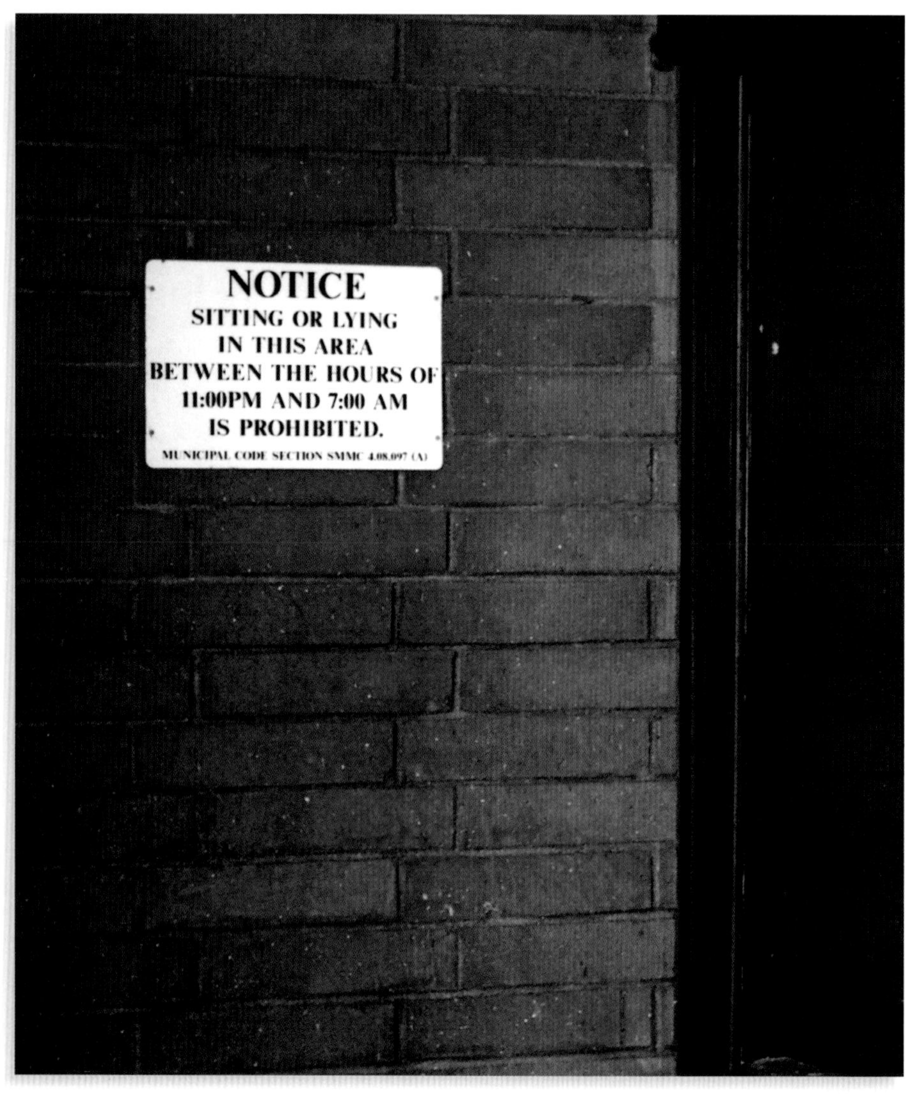

SANTA MONICA, CALIFORNIA

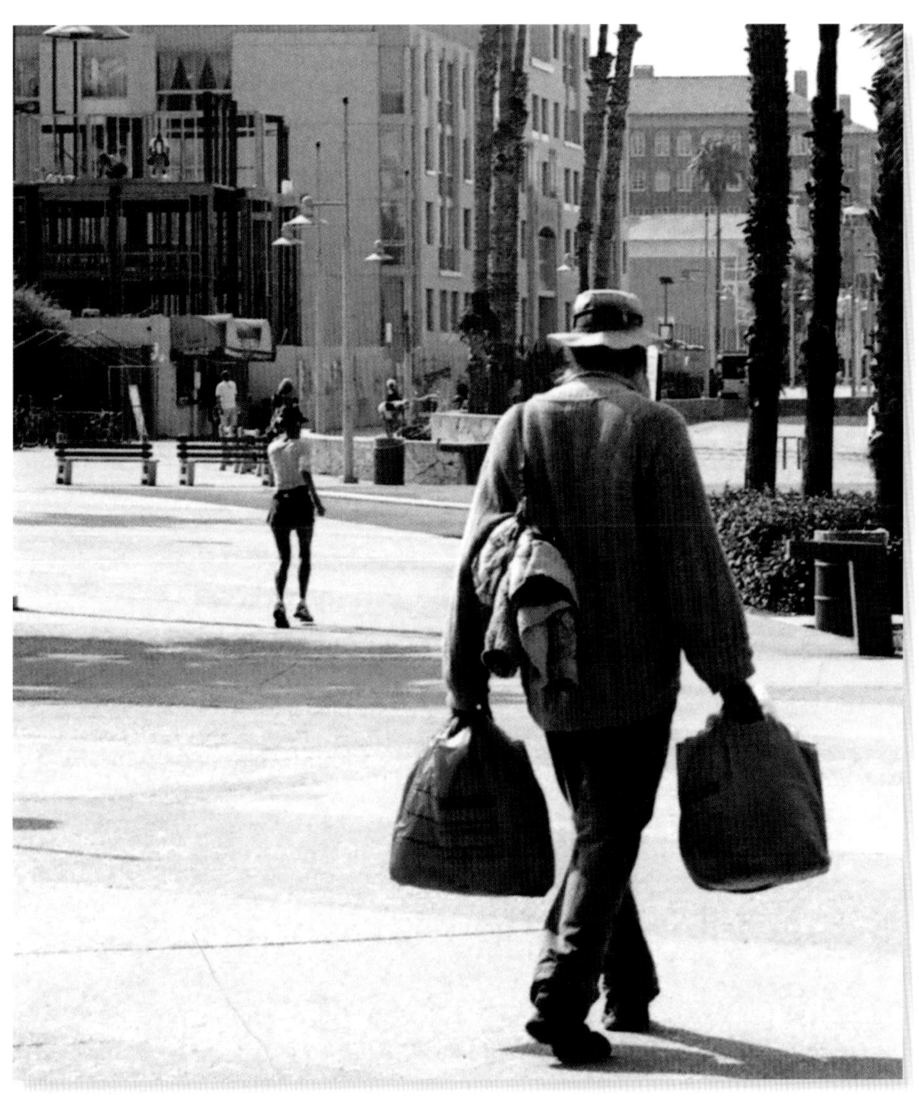

SANTA MONICA, CALIFORNIA

In talking with Bill Bickel, director of the Holy Family shelter in Indianapolis, it was suggested there be a blank picture, a blank page in this book for the homeless we don't so easily see…the mother and her children walking down the street, getting off the city bus, going to the family shelter.

We see the men at the mission, the women at the city park. But the homeless family staying at the shelter is not so obvious. She has spent the day looking for employment. The children have been in school. The father may or may not be staying at this shelter with them, but he too could be unemployed. And they return to the shelter for dinner and warmth for this night.

In a city of over 1 million people, there is only one shelter that has a capacity of sixteen families that will house a father, a mother and their children. Are we forcing the families to make decisions they would not otherwise make if the father could stay with his family? If my family were to lose our home, would I not sleep in a box so my children could sleep in a bed?

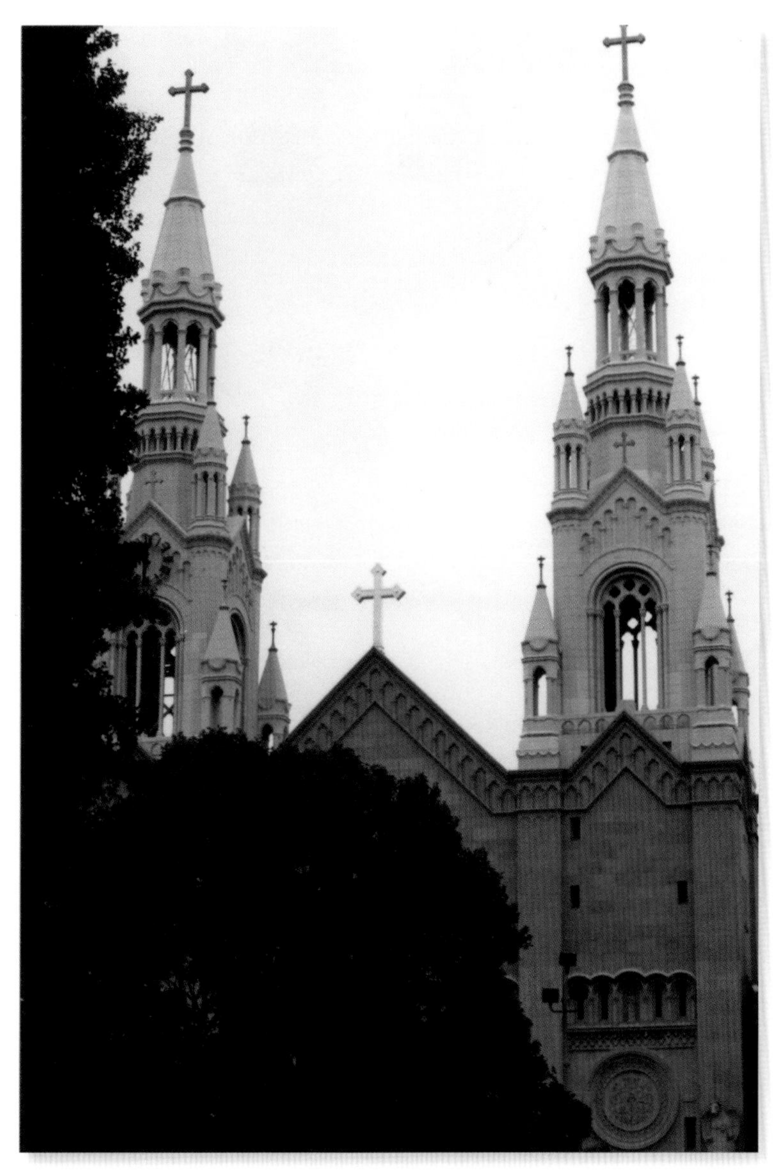

SAN FRANCISCO, CALIFORNIA

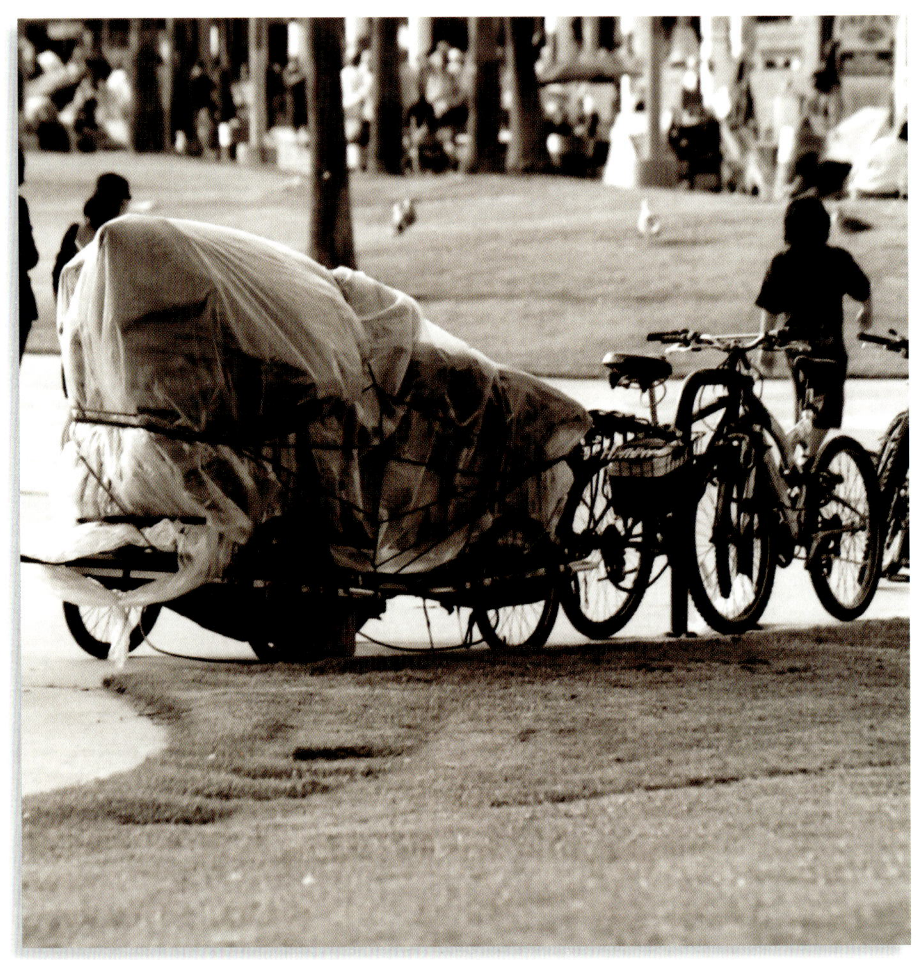

MUSCLE BEACH, CALIFORNIA

My friend asked him, "Is everything you have on that cart attached to the bike?"

"Yeah. Pretty simple life, huh?"

Carts are good. Some are quite creative. Of course there is the popular grocery store cart, but some carts are inventive.

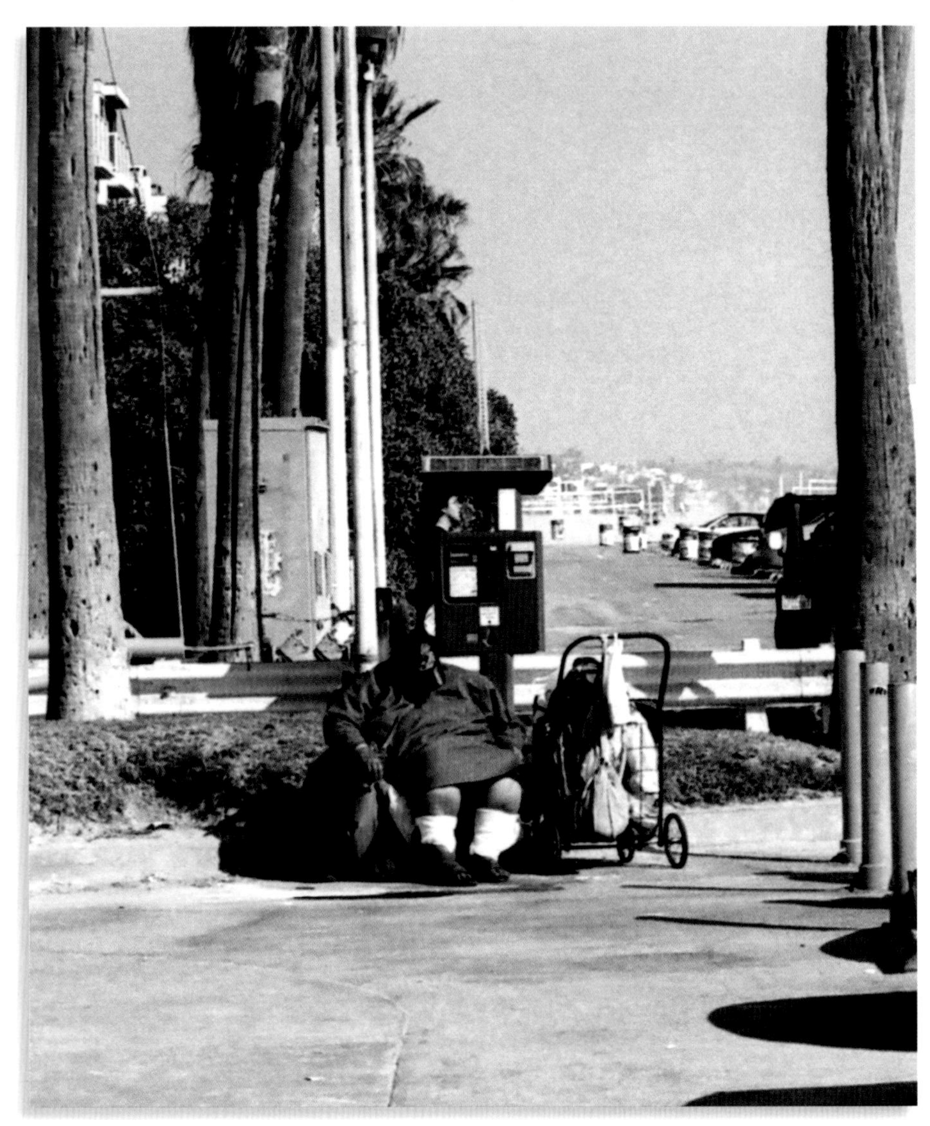

SANTA MONICA, CALIFORNIA

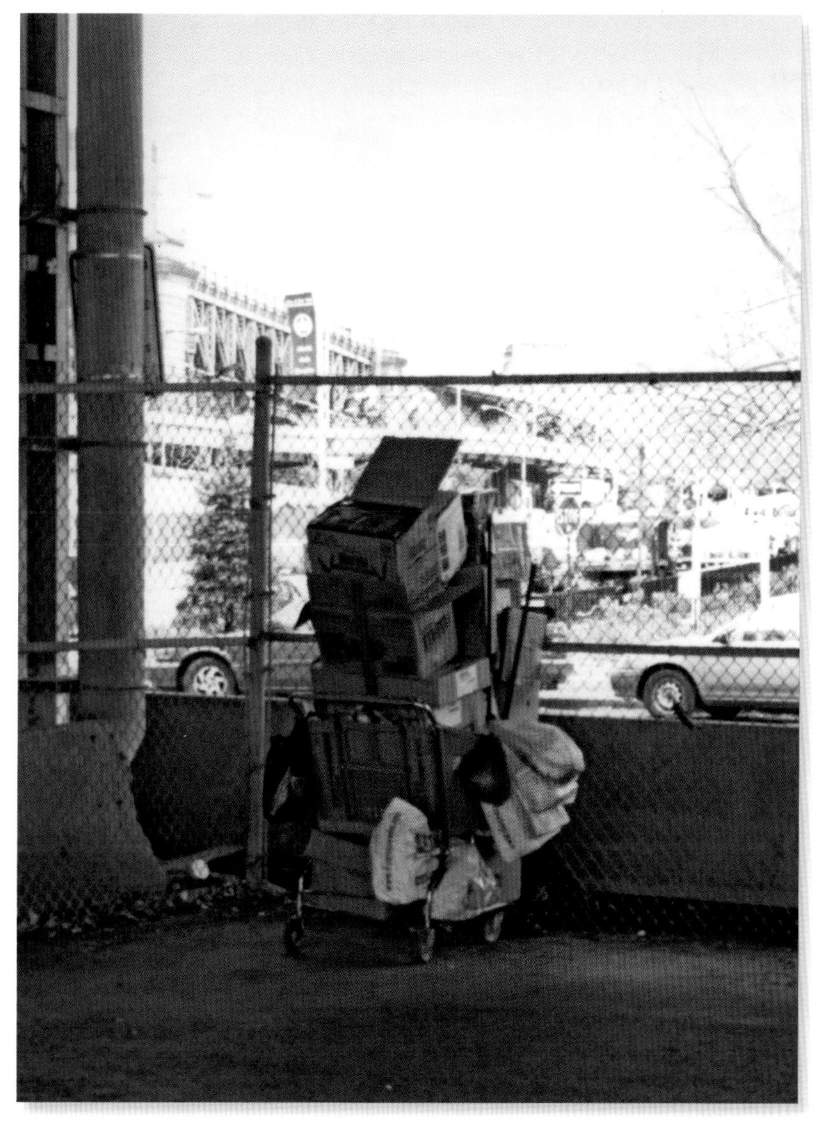

MANHATTAN, NEW YORK

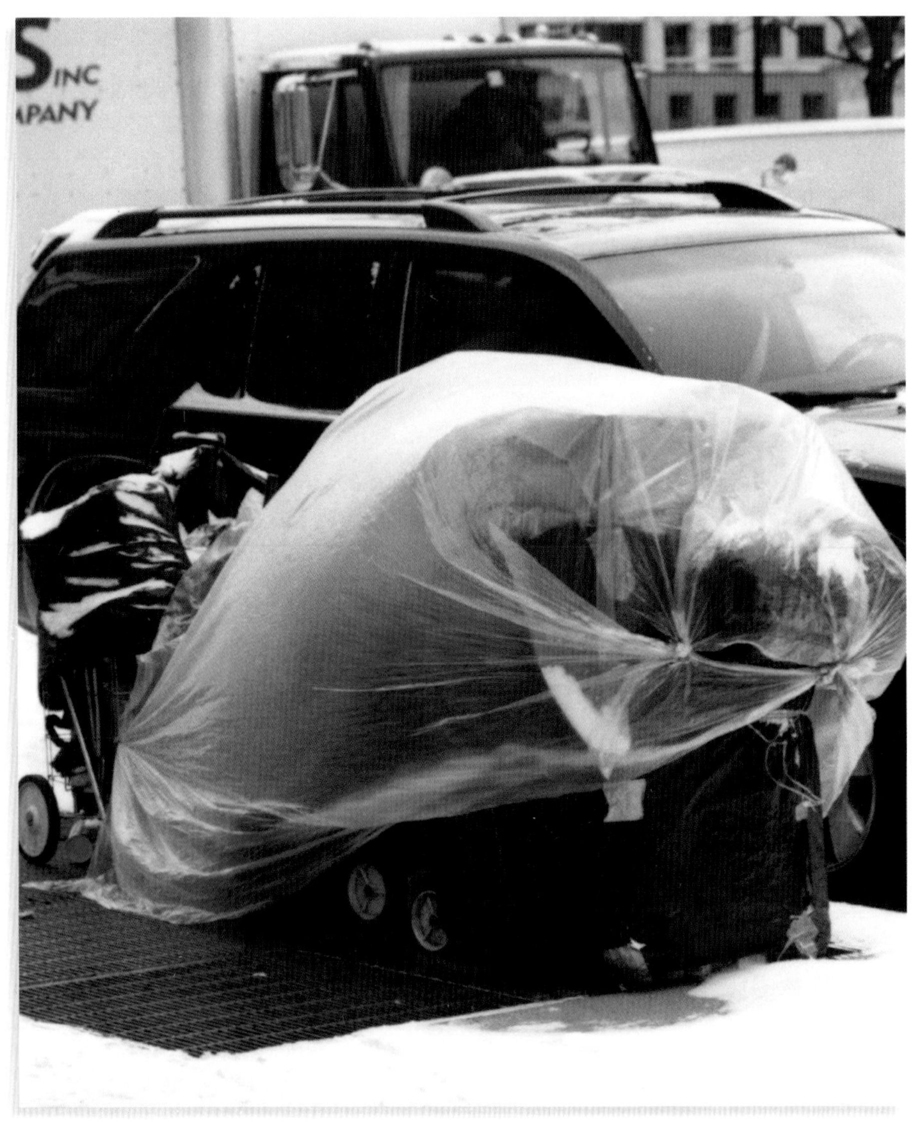

WASHINGTON, D.C.

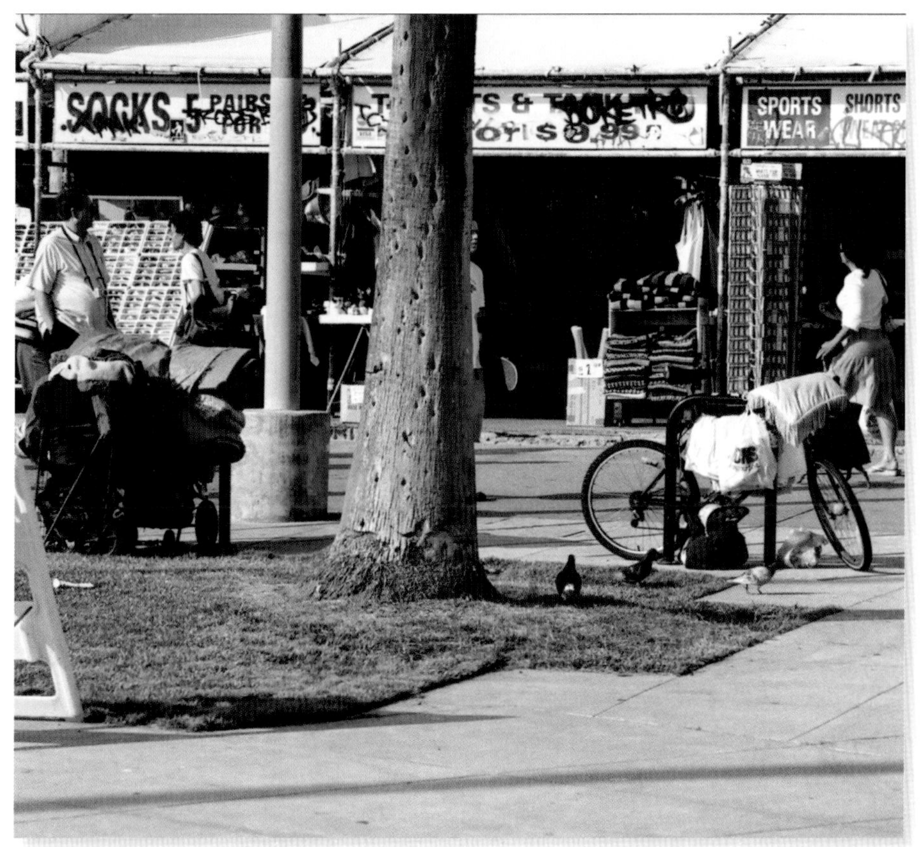

VENTURA BEACH, CALIFORNIA

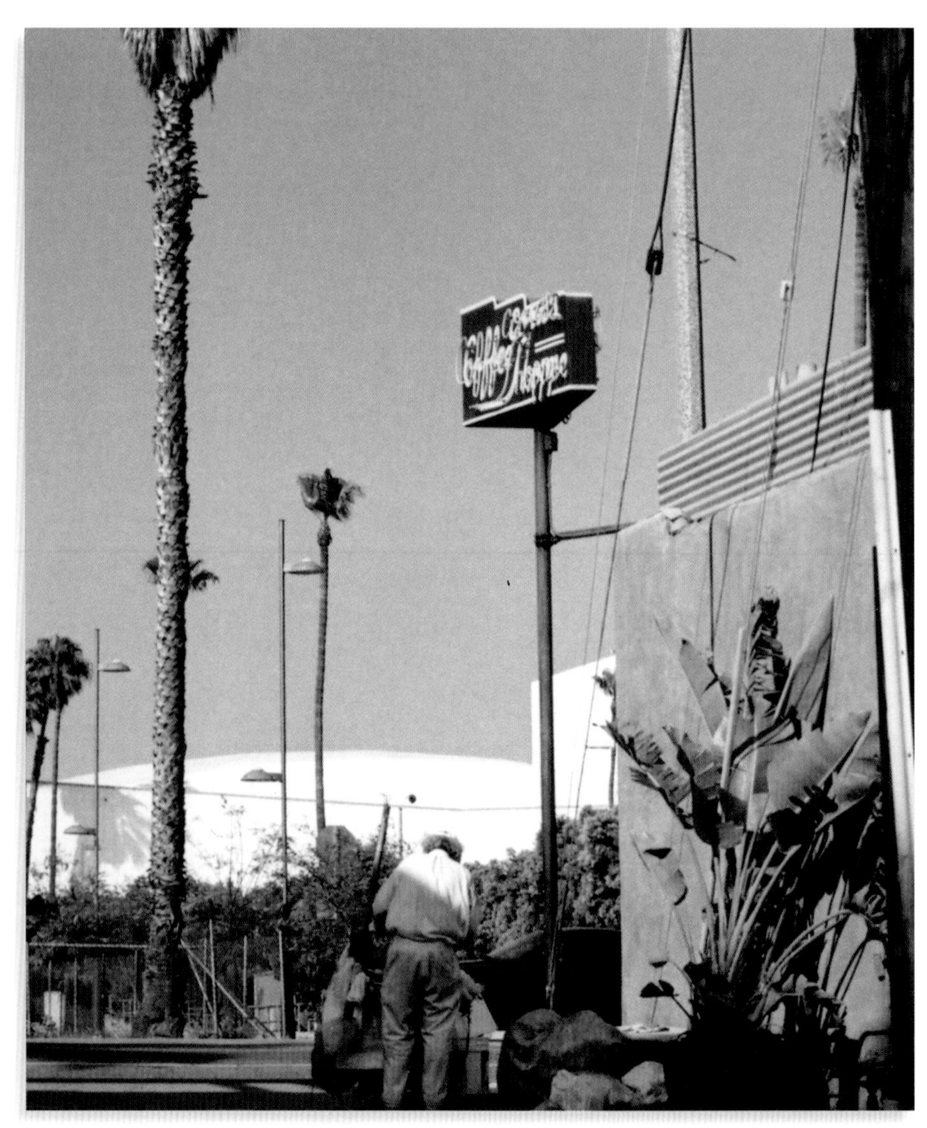

SANTA MONICA, CALIFORNIA

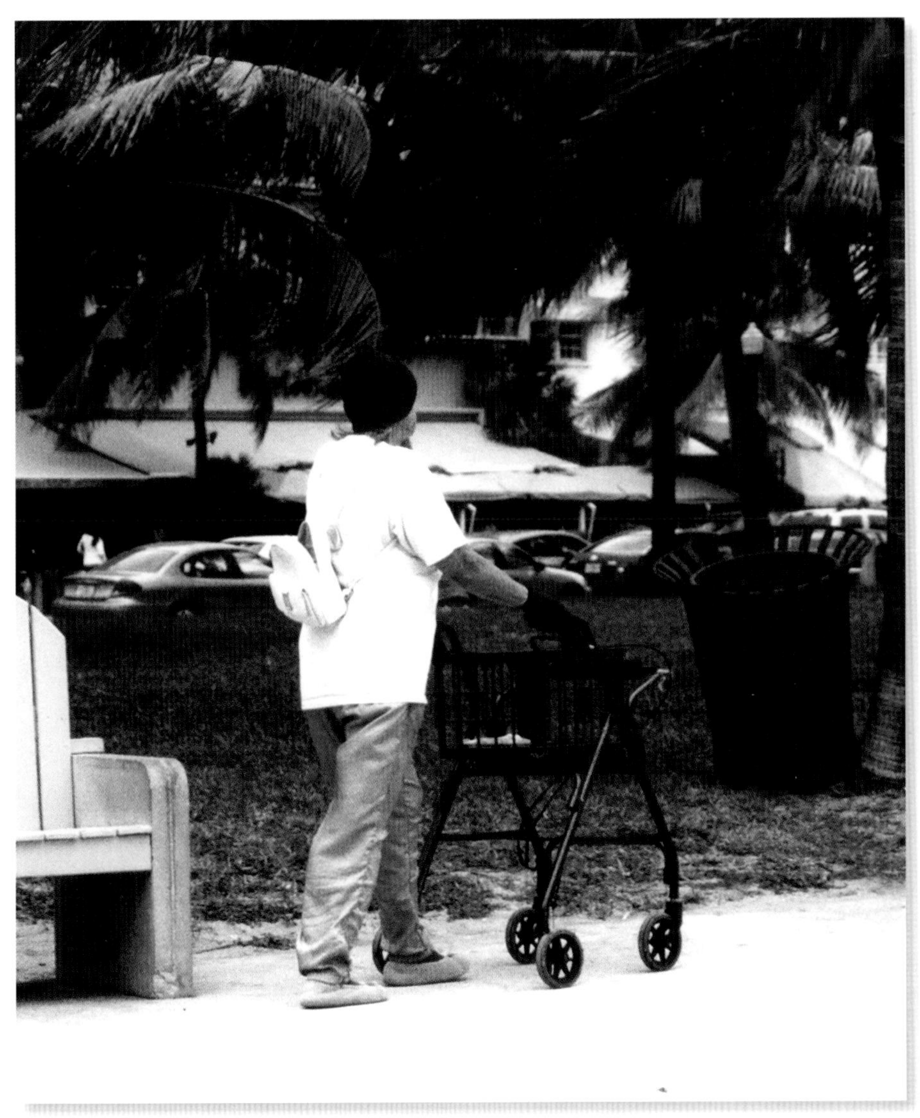

MIAMI, FLORIDA

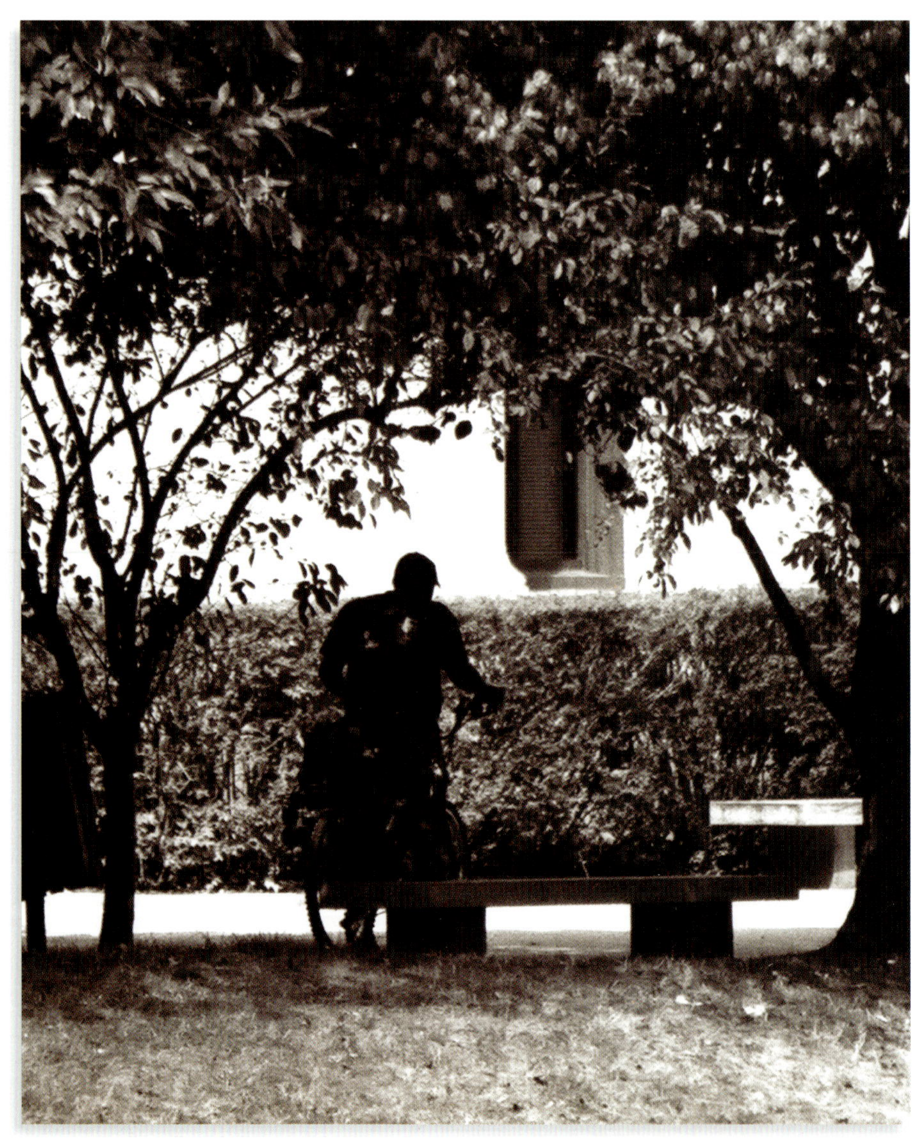

INDIANAPOLIS, INDIANA

I stopped at the Salvation Army one morning on the way to work to deliver a check. I handed it to the man at the desk and explained that I would like the funds earmarked for the Florida hurricane relief efforts. The Salvation Army was doing tremendous work helping those devastated by the four hurricanes that had gone through the state.

"Thanks," he said, "I'll make sure it is put to good use." I turned and left, heading for a diner in Speedway to have breakfast.

The people at the restaurant all know me, as I frequently have meals there. Mike, the manager, and the others at the counter greeted me when I placed my order. Fred, the elderly man who works in the dining room came over and talked with me as I ate breakfast. Nice people.

It was a beautiful, crisp October morning and the sun was shining.

A man rode up on an old mountain bike. He was dressed in cargo shorts and a green t-shirt with the sleeves cut off, and hiking boots that had seen the real trail. A bandana covered his hair and there was a small bundle strapped over the rear wheel with a teddy bear riding backwards to keep him company. He leaned the old Marin bike against the building and came to the front counter, asking for the manager. The biker's tanned legs and arms were lean, yet muscular, the way a body gets from many miles on the saddle.

Mike went to the customer side of the counter and listened to the man. Then he went to the kitchen area and came back with a big breakfast and a cup of coffee. The man thanked him and sat on the opposite side of the dining area from me.

The bike's seat was padded and worn. The Marin was in good shape but showed the results of being ridden, handlebar pads and wheels displaying real use, not just the evidence of casual riding in the neighborhood.

I approached Mike and asked about his conversation with the rider. "He said he was the indigent biker going from Seattle to Sarasota. He asked if I would let him have breakfast. He told me he had ridden from Crawfordsville this morning. That's sixty miles and it's only 9:30."

I approached his table and sat down uninvited. He looked at me with clear blue eyes as I commented on his bicycle. He continued eating and explained the bike was old, but rode well.

"I saw you talking to Mike and I was interested."

"He's a good guy. A lot of people don't understand," the rider said.

"Doug," he said, offering his hand in welcome. "David," I replied.

"How was it getting through the Rockies?" I asked. I had done some bike riding of my own, but nothing like his trip.

"I went the northern route, through Idaho and the Dakotas, so it wasn't bad. The hardest part was Iowa, with the long rolling hills. They were difficult."

He looked to be in his late thirties or early forties. His voice was calm, his demeanor at ease.

"What's your story?" I asked.

"A man who meant the world to me, my greatest friend, died. He and I were helping people move furniture after Hurricane Charlie and my friend had a heart attack. His mother lives in Seattle, so I had him cremated and took him to her. I live in Florida and I am on my way back. This was the only way I could afford to get there."

We talked a little more and I stood to leave. We shook hands again.

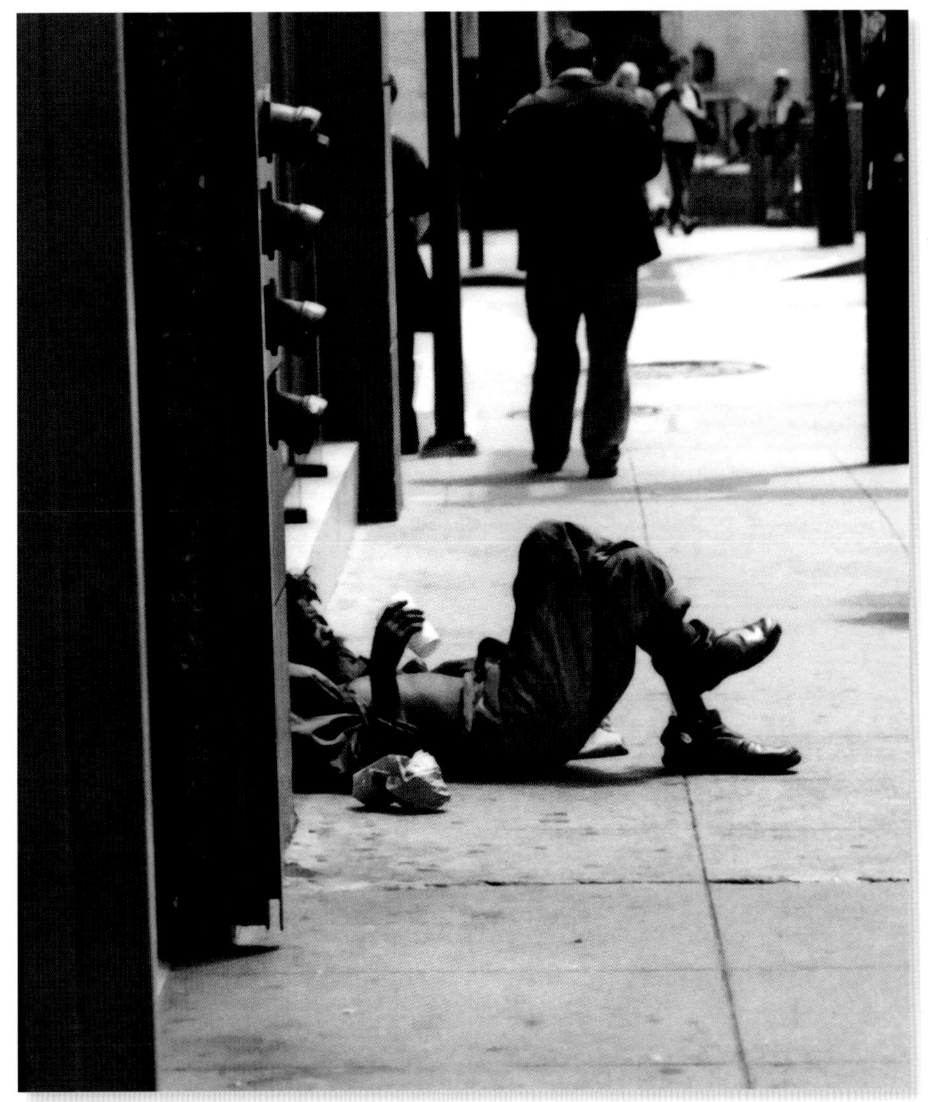

Living large in San Francisco

SAN FRANCISCO, CALIFORNIA

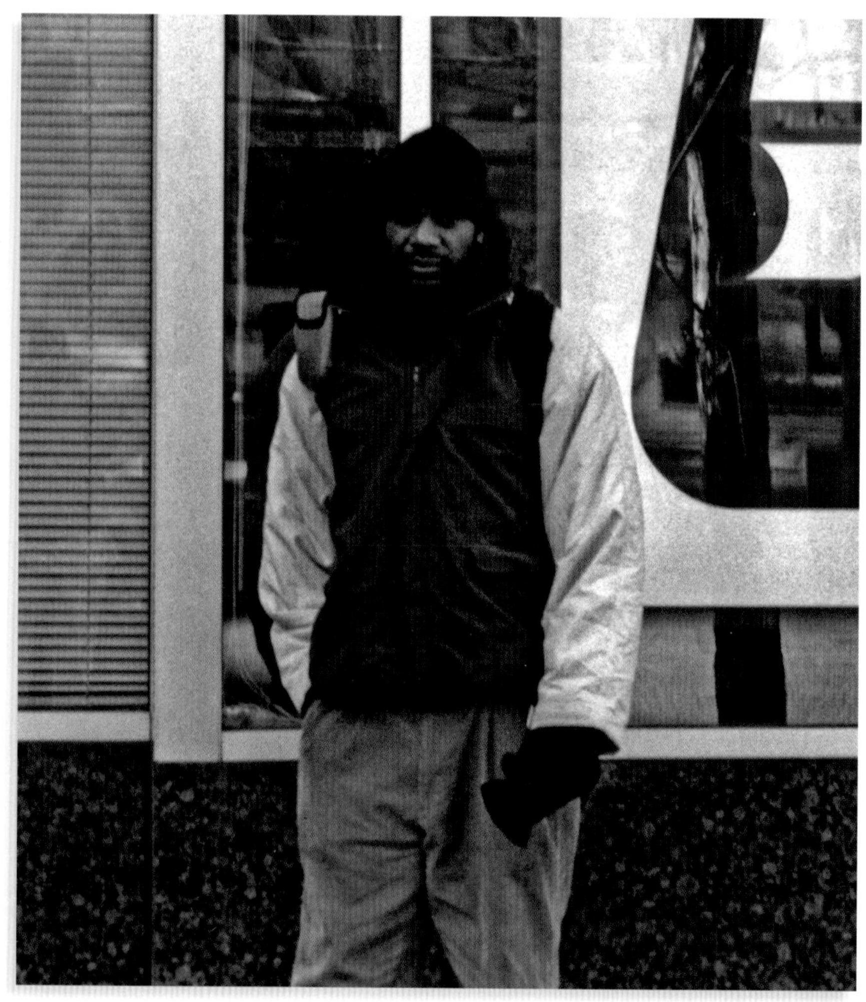

"How did you become homeless?"

"I don't know," came the reply.

INDIANAPOLIS, INDIANA

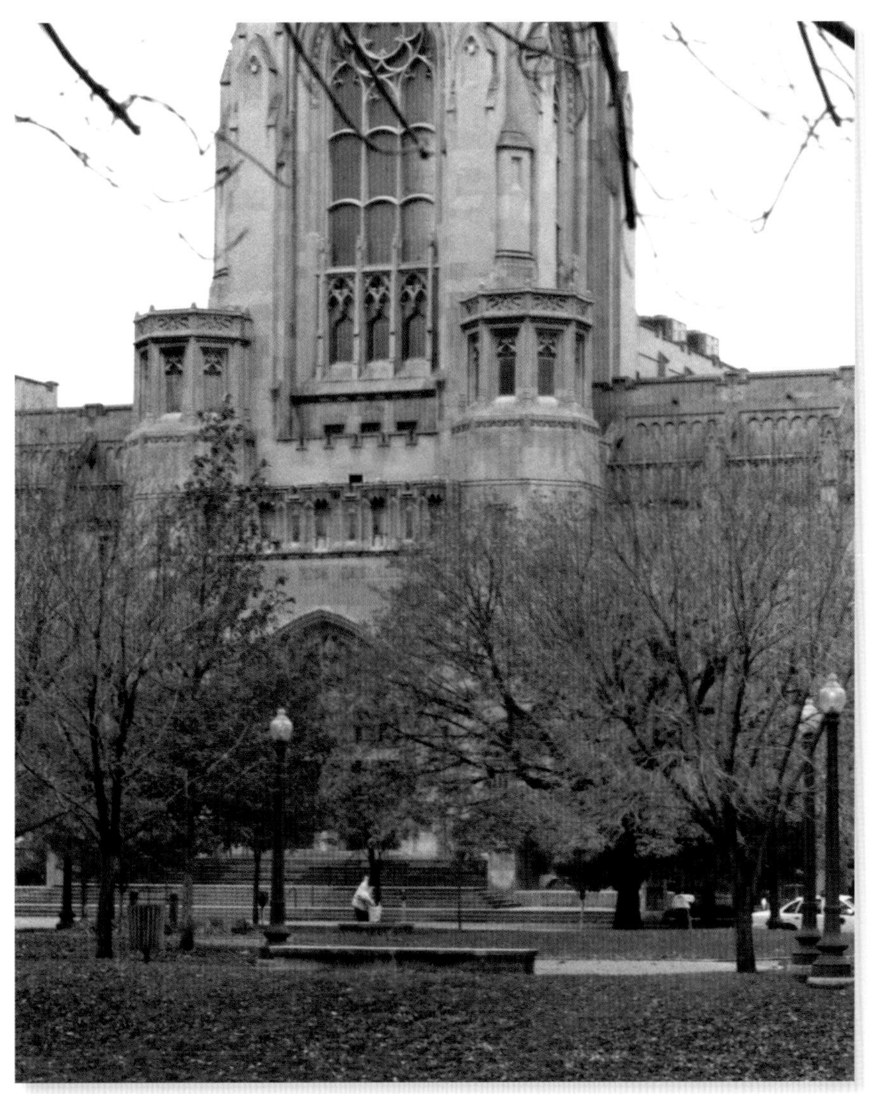

INDIANAPOLIS, INDIANA

Religions have held for thousands of years that there is a spirit of One greater than any of us, that exists in each of us. How we cultivate that spirit, how we celebrate that spirit, how we are used by that spirit varies in as many ways as there have been people over the years. It is thought that all of us share a oneness in this respect.

Can we see that spirit, that piece of ourselves, in this man?

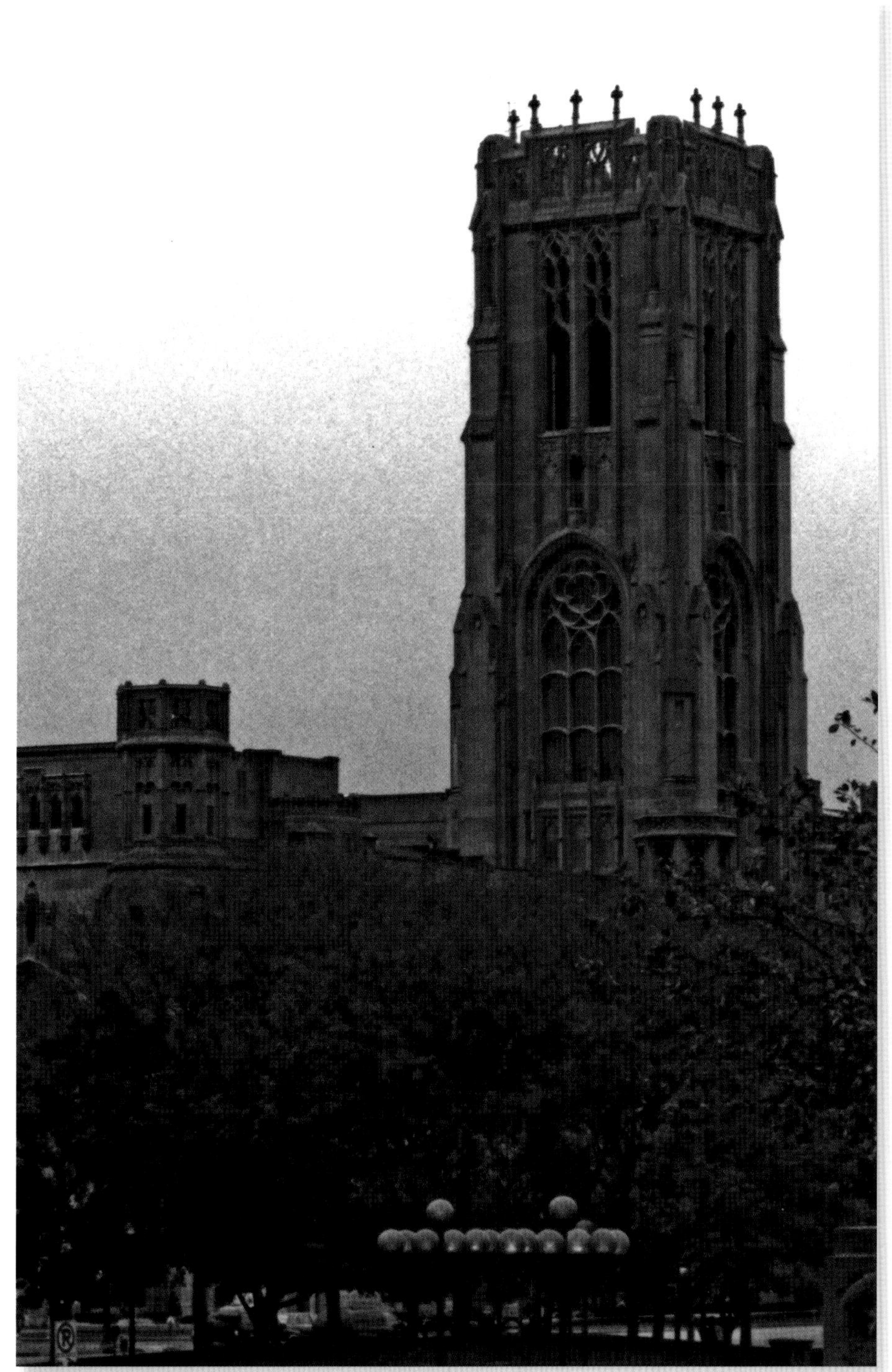

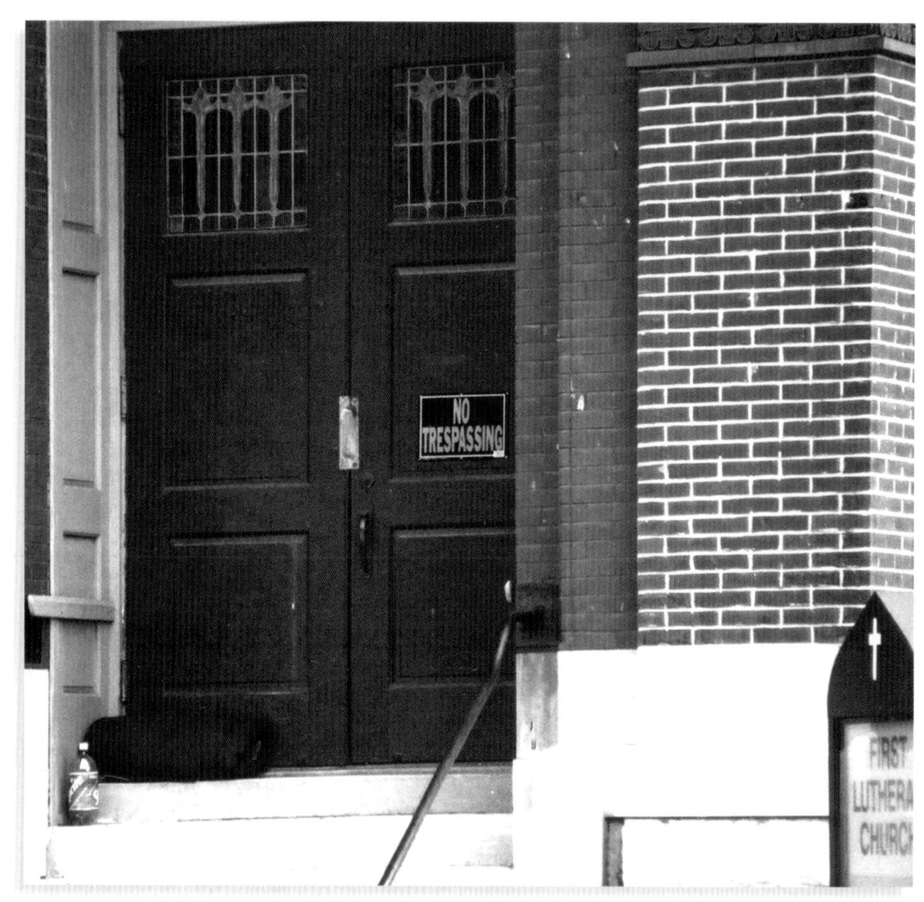

INDIANAPOLIS, INDIANA

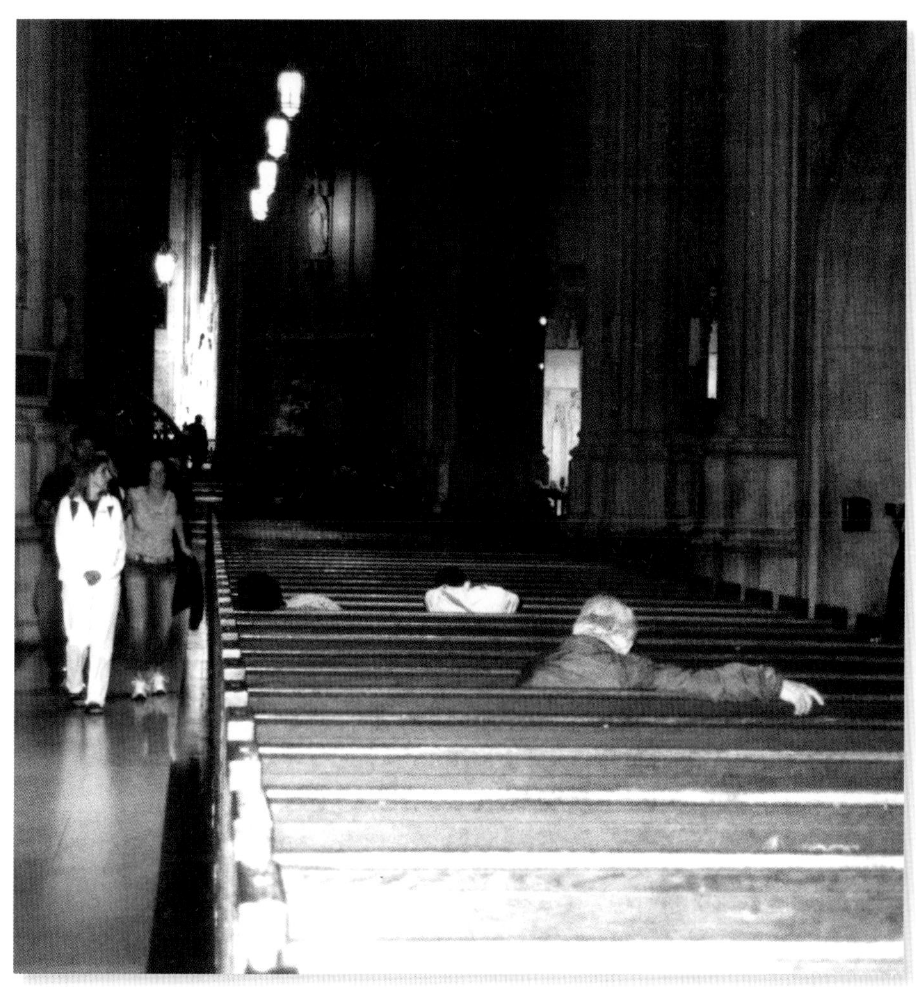

NEW YORK CITY, NEW YORK

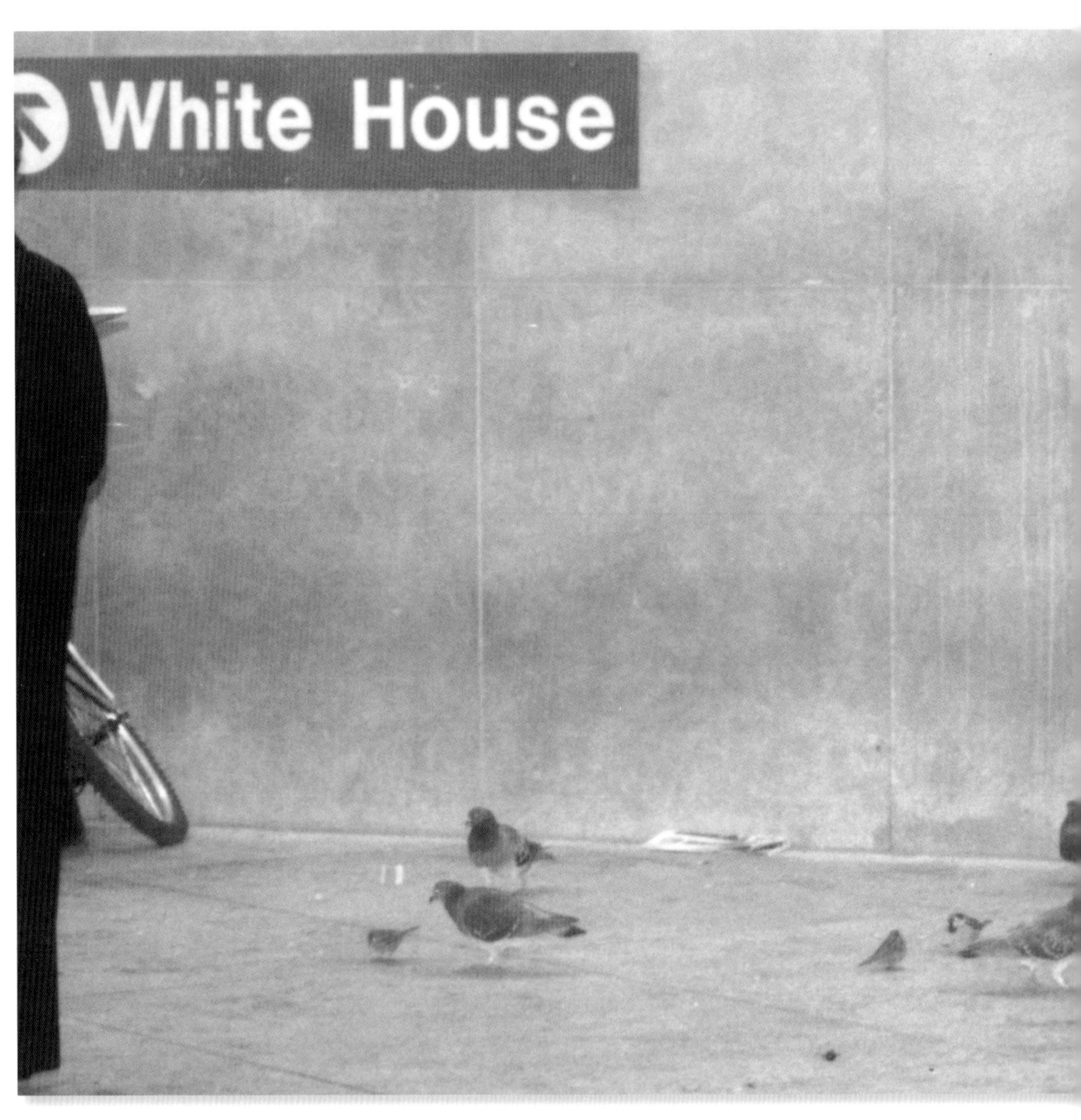

This was funny.

Okay, maybe funny is the wrong word.

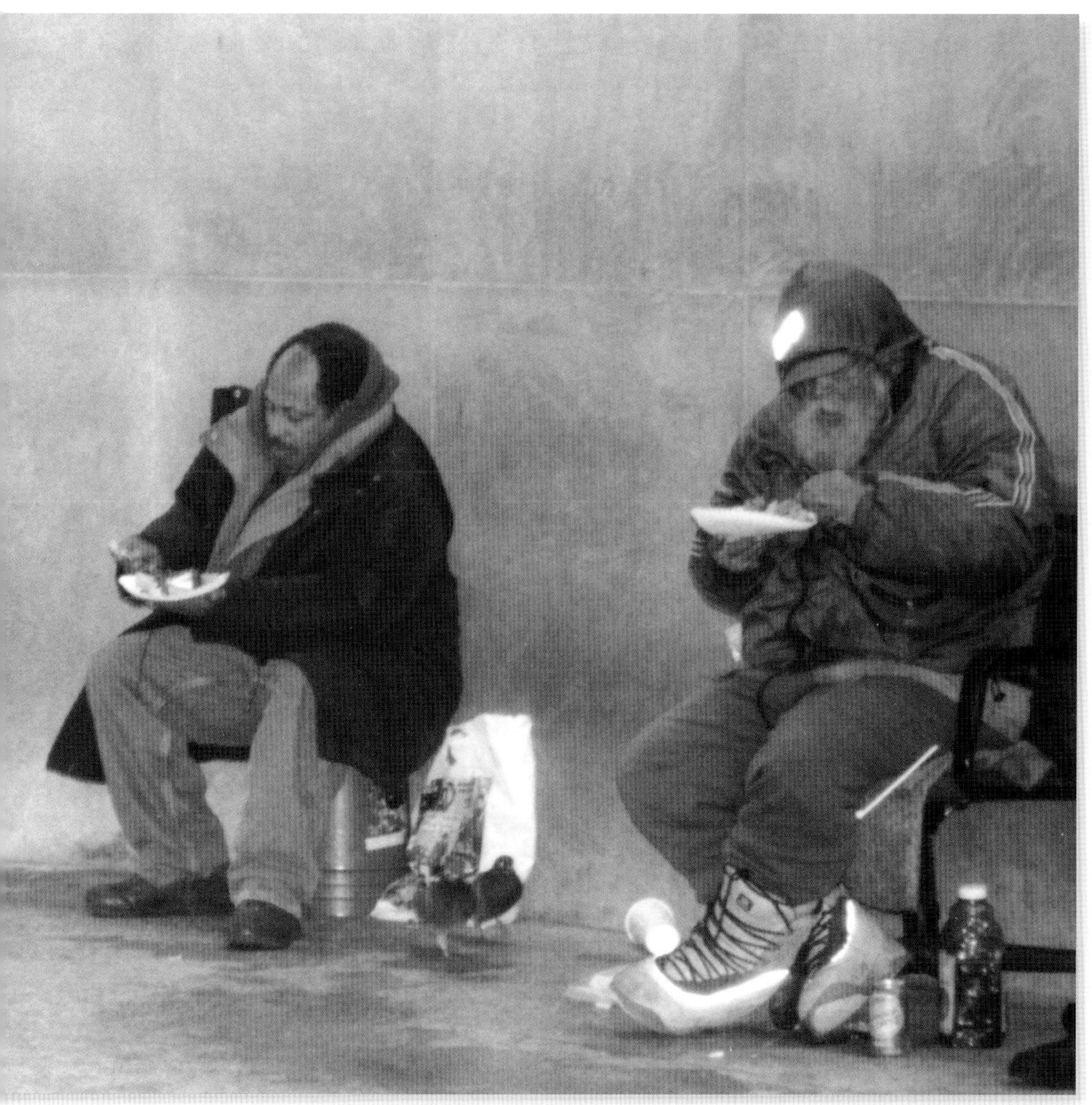

Ladies in fur coats brought desserts to the men from an inaugural party near the White House in Washington, D.C. The men living there feed the pigeons.

Outside the entrance to McPherson Square Station, a blizzard rages.

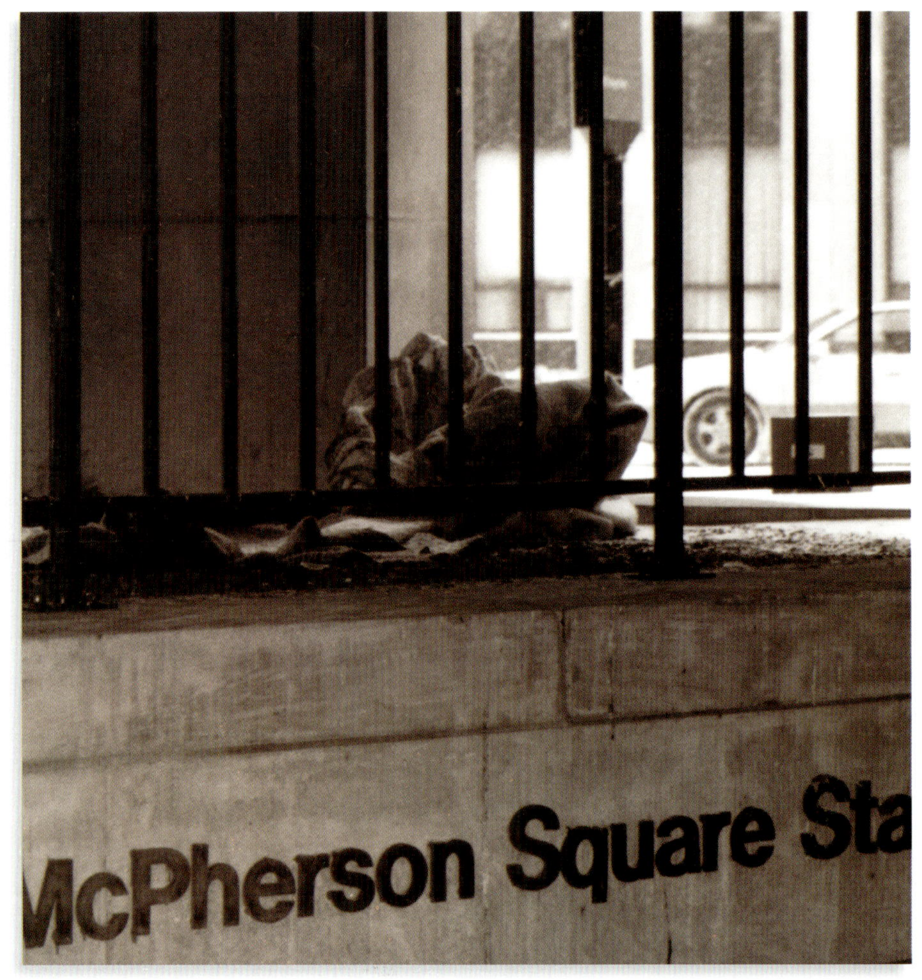

WASHINGTON, D.C.

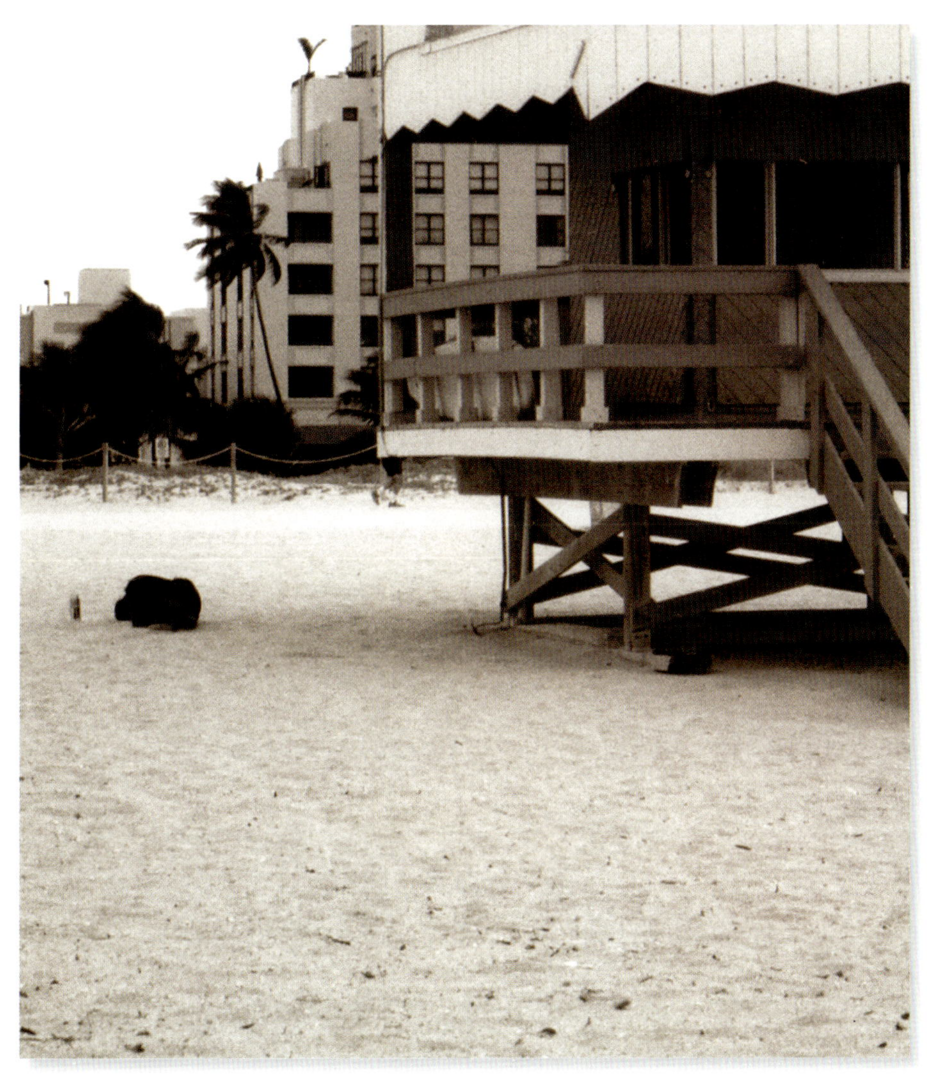

MIAMI, FLORIDA

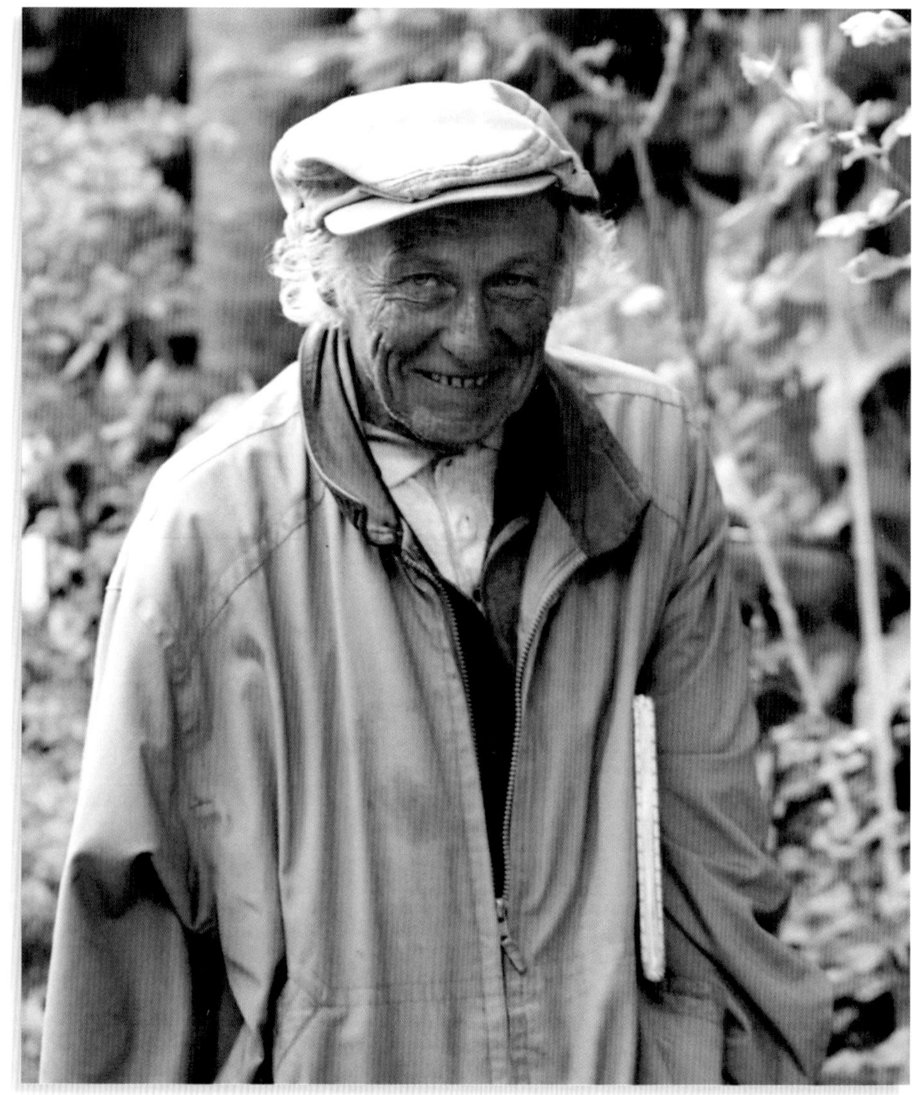

"Excuse me, do you have a quarter I could have?" The voice was quiet, respectful, maybe even a little shy. He was an older man but I was hard-pressed to guess an age.

"I'll give you a little more than that if I may take your picture."

"Sure, that would be good." The camera captured his interesting face, the little man with a writing tablet under his arm. There was a kindness in his eyes, a vitality.

"Would you like to see my art?" He gestured to the notebook. I told him I would be honored if he would share it with me. The drawings were sporadic and childlike on the worn pages.

"Do you know where I started to draw?"

"No, where?"

"I was in the meat packing industry for thirty years, but I started to draw when I was in prison."

I didn't ask why he was in prison. We talked a few more minutes and I gave him some money.

"This is my lucky day," he said before we parted.

I felt the same way.

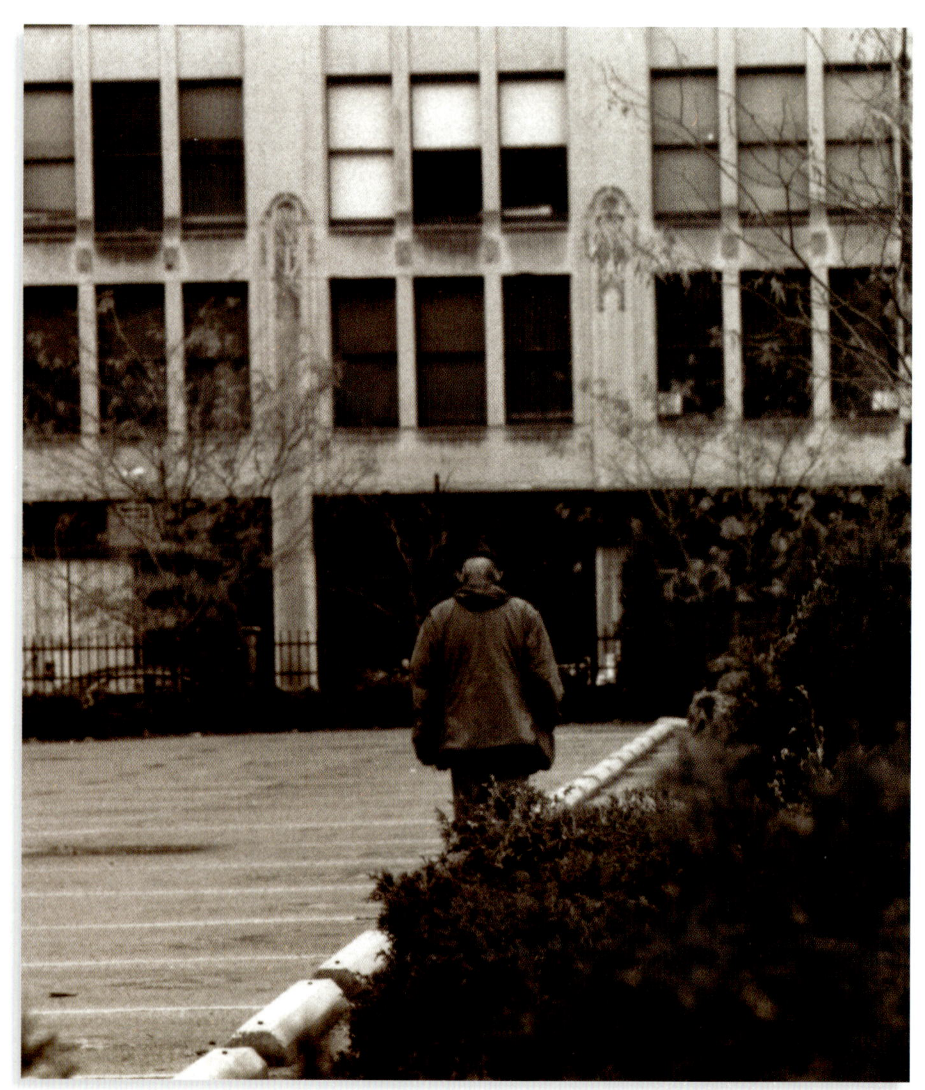

INDIANAPOLIS, INDIANA

I stood at the bus stop downtown smoking a cigarette. A man with a black eye approached and asked if I had one to spare. "Sure," I replied.

He told me a story. "I had a little extra last night, so I bought a bottle and went to an alley to drink it. Two other guys, guys I knew, saw where I was headed and I drank with them. Gave them what I could. Then they beat me up and took everything. Next time I have something to drink, I'm doing it alone."

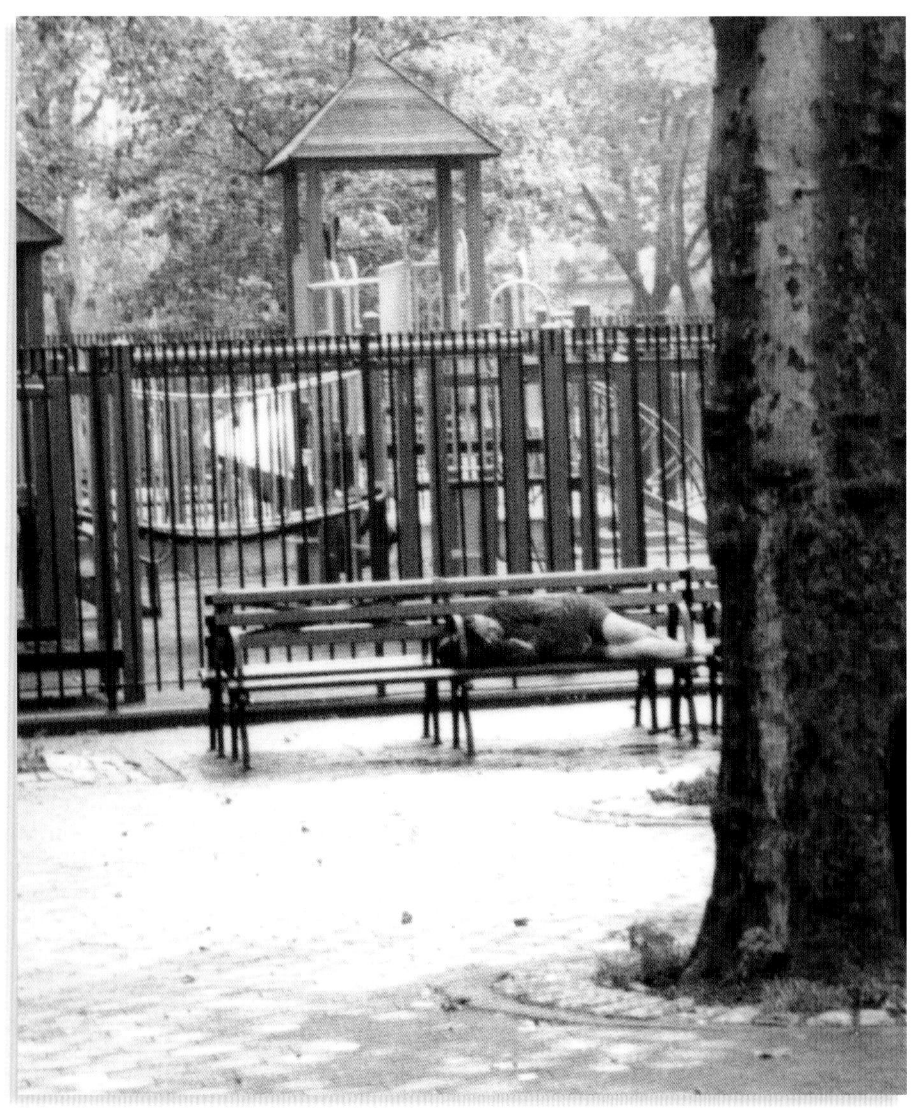

SOHO, NEW YORK

Fourteen. Living out of a dumpster. More terrified of the abuse in her parents' home than life alone on the streets.

How do we see her when she begs for money?

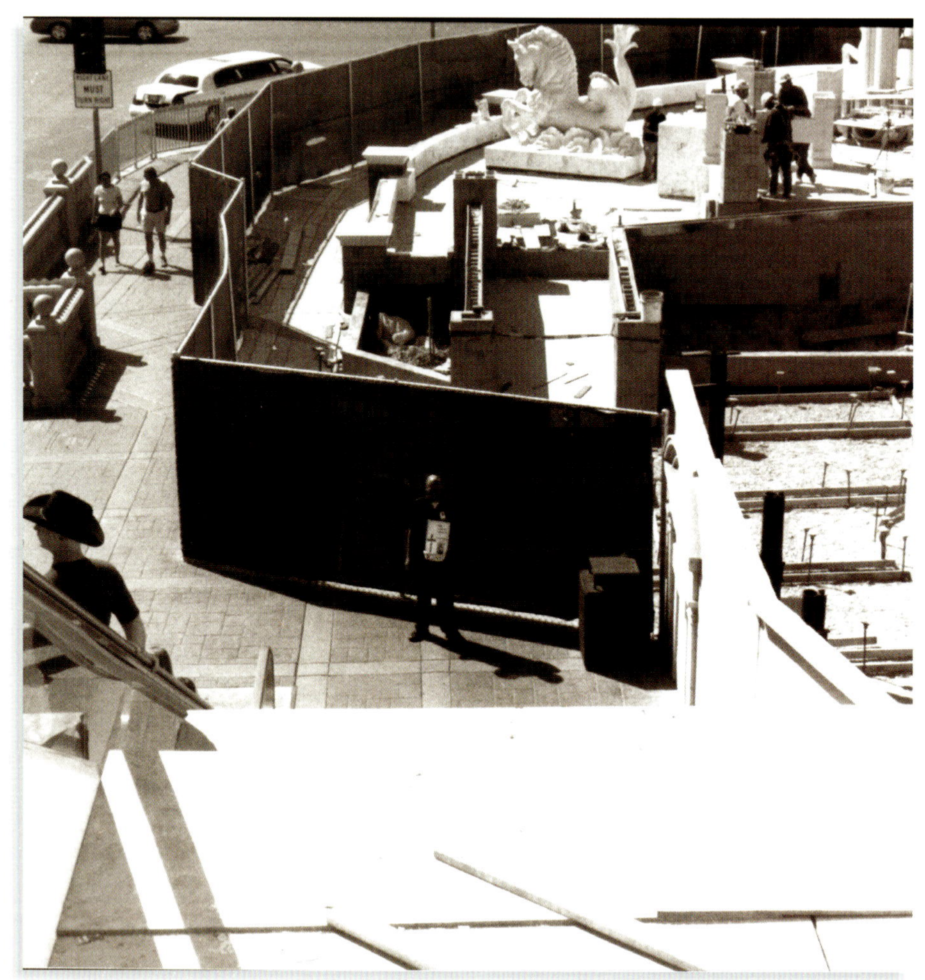

LAS VEGAS, NEVADA

Vegas and Orlando

Homeless people are hard to find on the Las Vegas strip and in Orlando. You know they are there…somewhere.

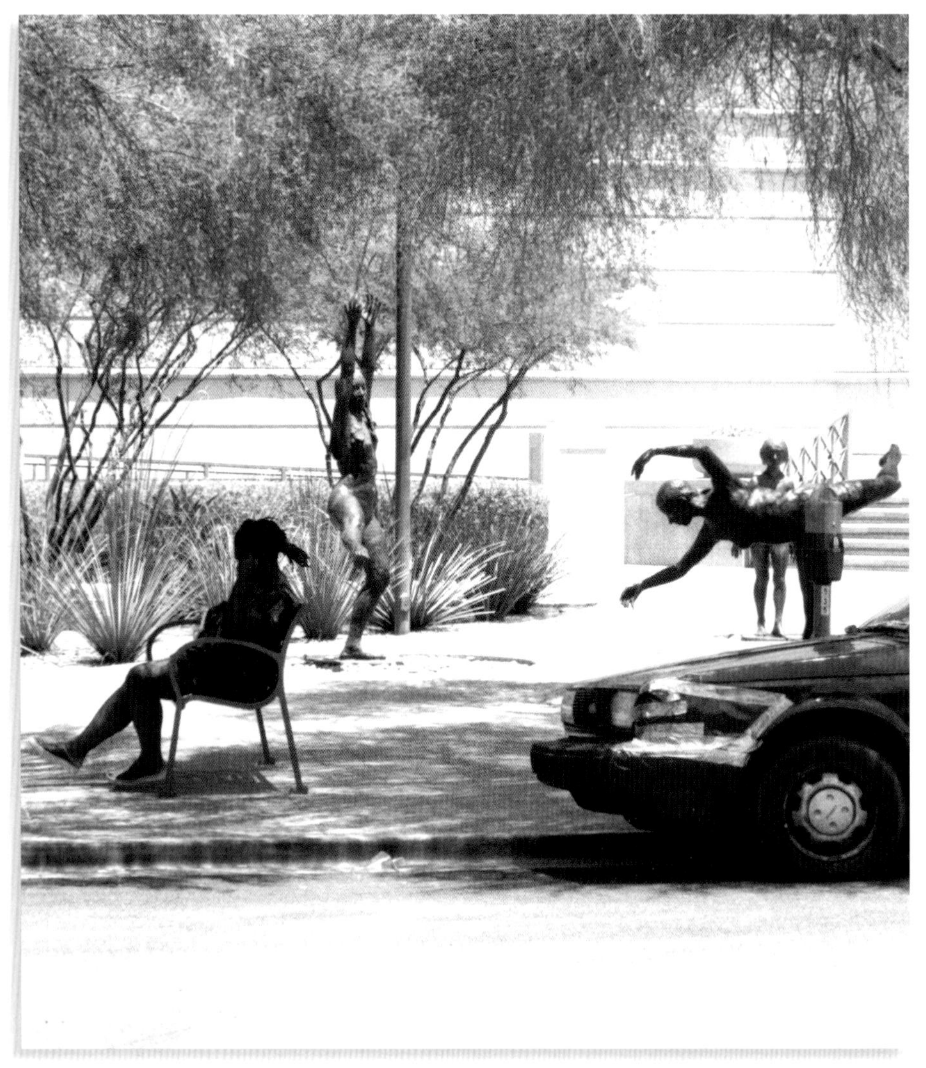

PHOENIX, ARIZONA

As posed as one of the statues nearby, she sits quietly on a warm Phoenix day. But the grace of the statues is gone from her; instead dejection resides within her heart.

Where does she turn now?

CINCINNATI, OHIO

Tonight there is a man confronted with his mortality. He waits for the darkness, fear overcoming him. Knowing that he cannot stay awake for the safety of the morning light.

Where does he rest? Most of the time, he is able to remain alert at night, guarding himself against the insistent predators of his homeless world. And at daybreak, he can sleep in the relative peace of the city park.

But not tonight. He is tired and hungry. The day did not go well. Every time he was almost asleep, he would be rousted. There was a special event in town and the officials wanted all of them to be out of sight. So he moved from place to place, never feeling comfortable he would be allowed to stay.

As night falls, as the city celebrates around him, where will he be safe?

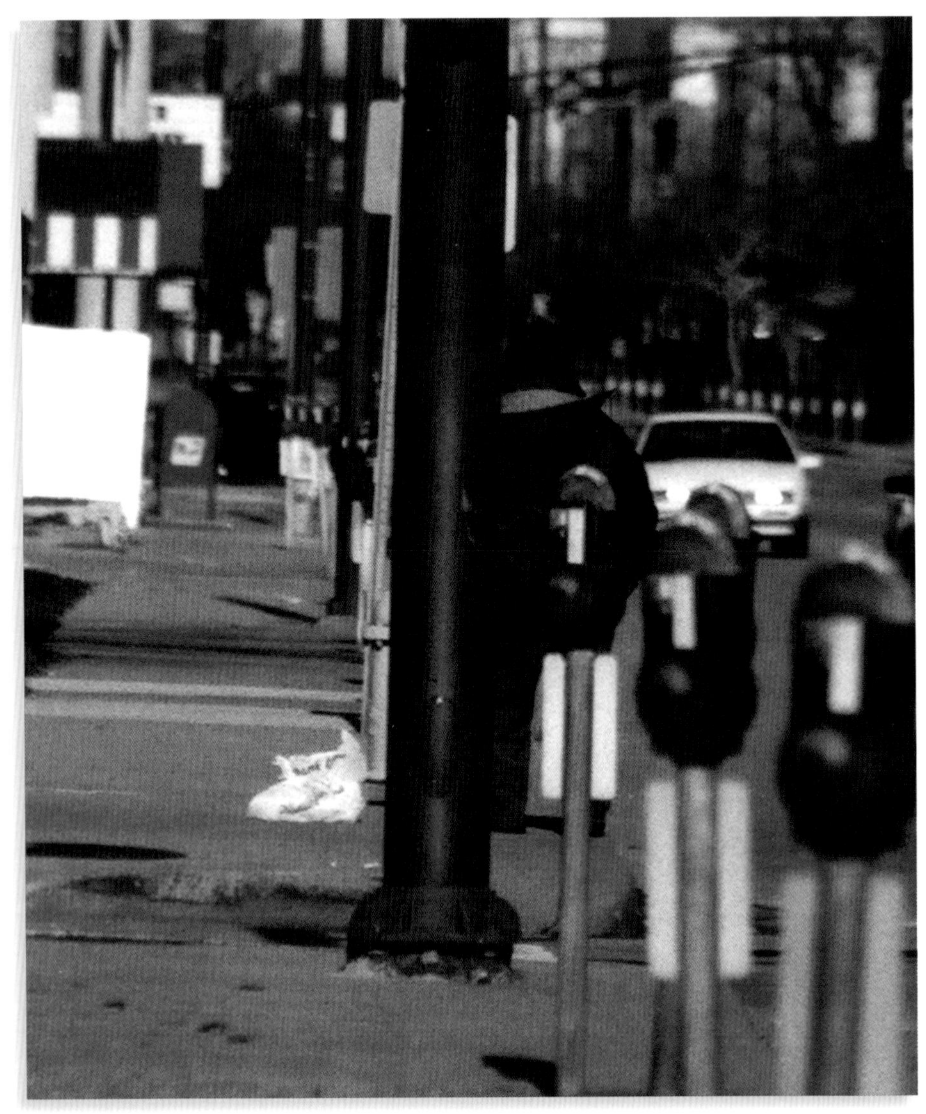

INDIANAPOLIS, INDIANA

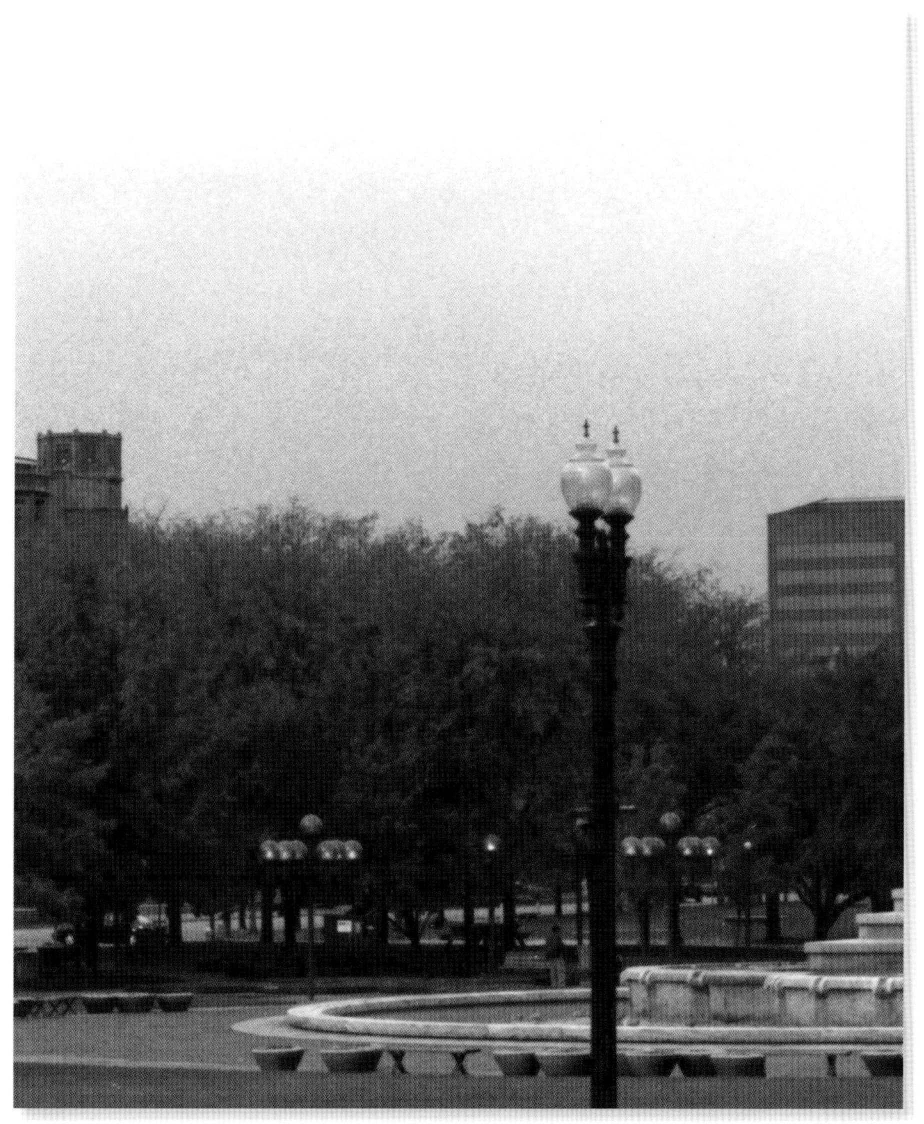

INDIANAPOLIS, INDIANA

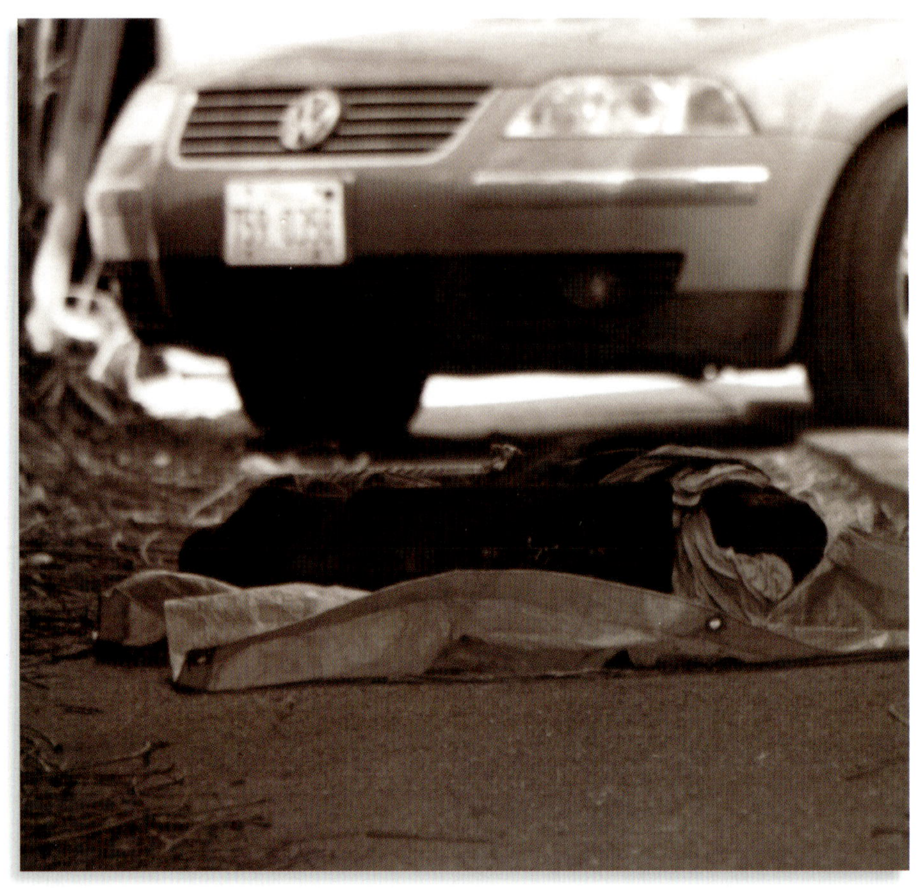

CHICAGO, ILLINOIS

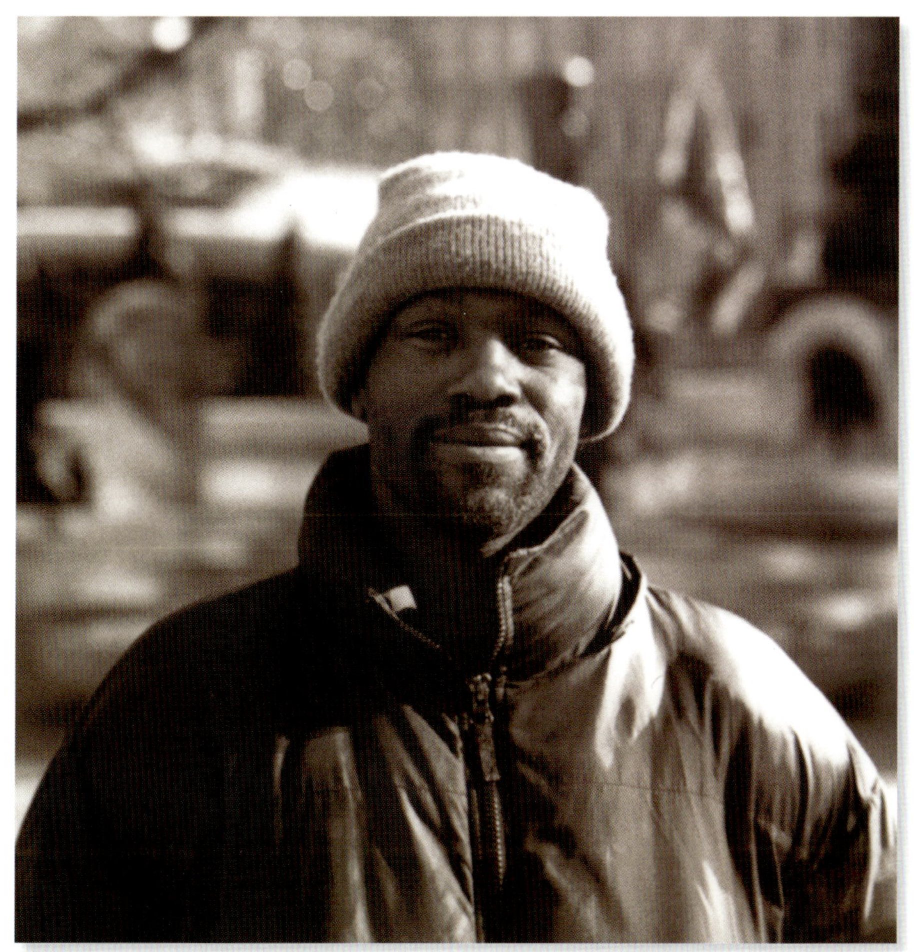

Back to back. Nothing in common. Everything in common.

Like me and them. Like you and them.

All of us share the common humanity.

INDIANAPOLIS, INDIANA

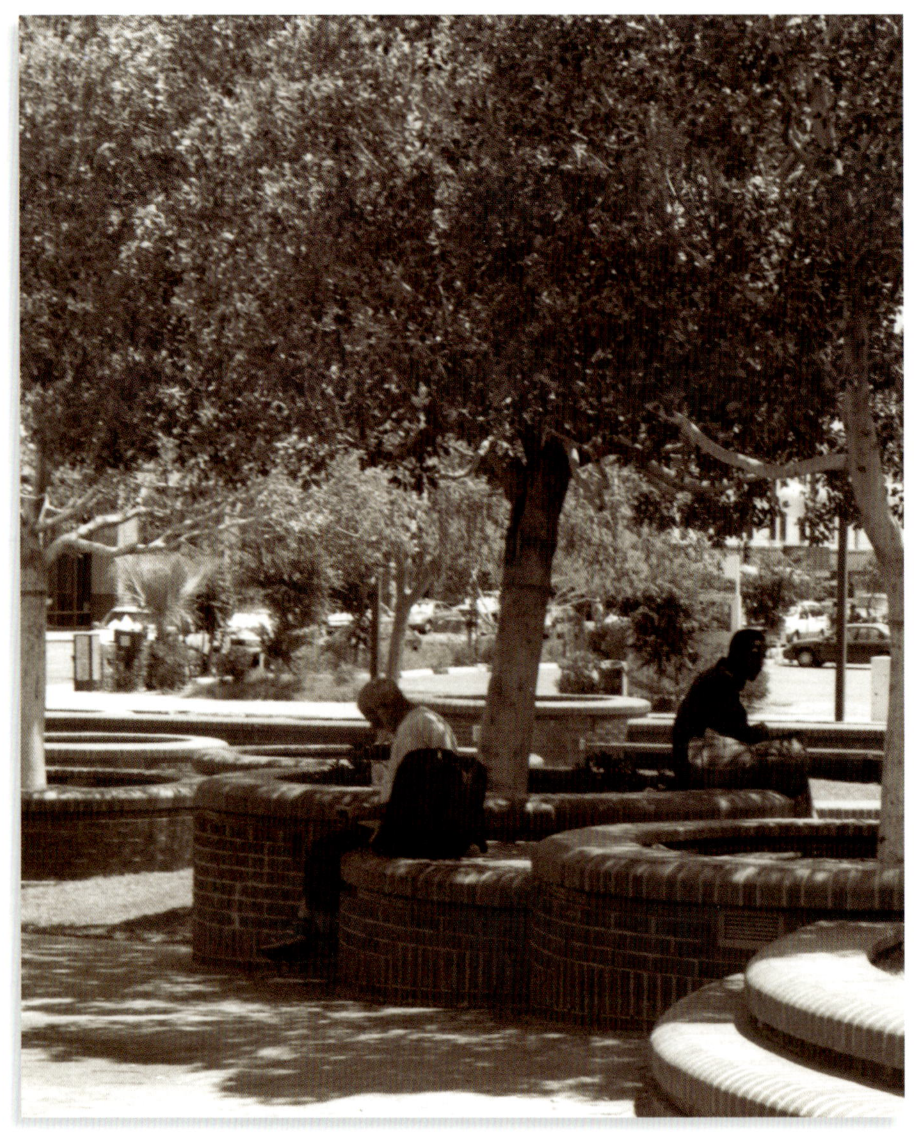

Very few shelters allow men to stay with their families.

INDIANAPOLIS, INDIANA

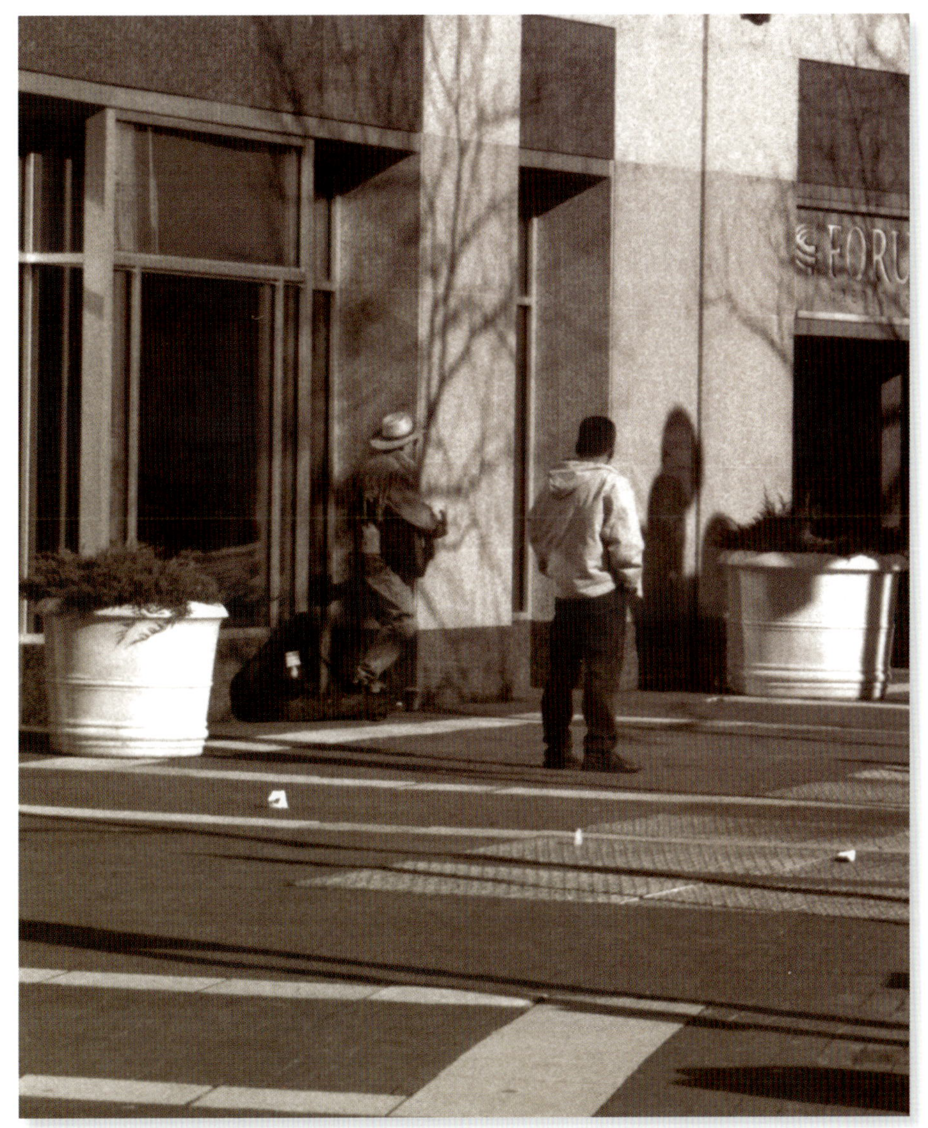

Do homeless fathers love their children less?

INDIANAPOLIS, INDIANA

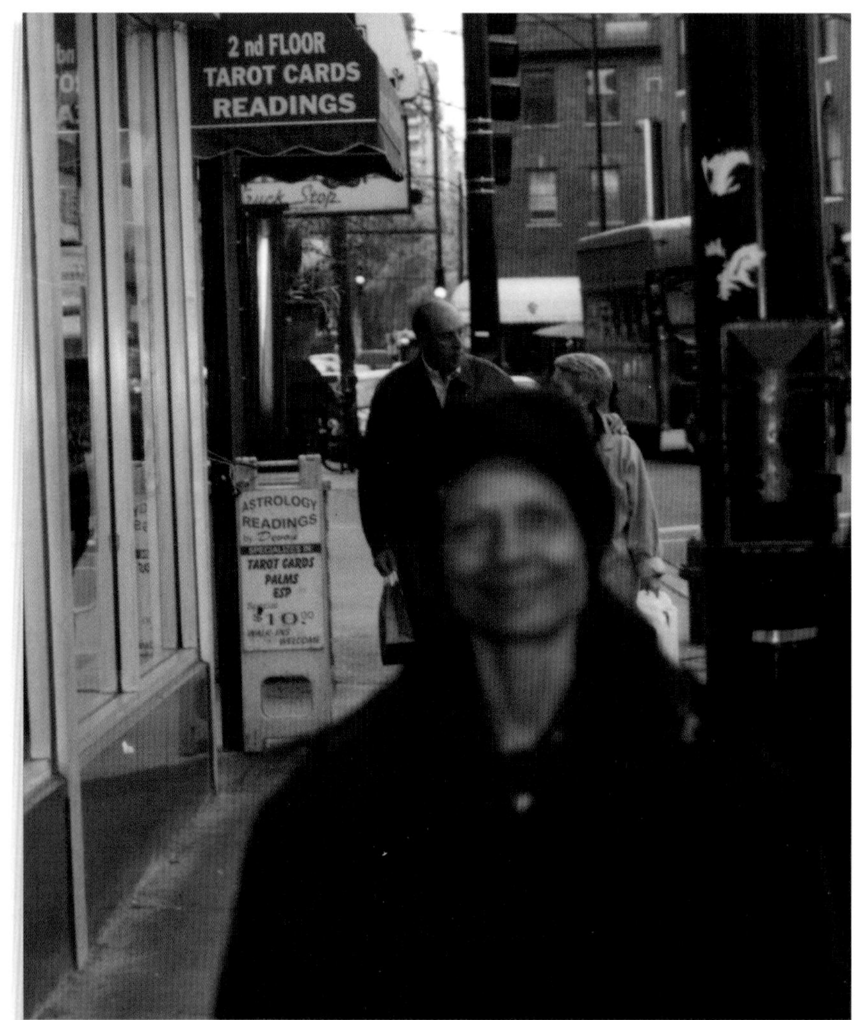

"Hey Mister, do you have a job?"

"Yes, I have a job."

"Can you get me a job?"

"My job is far from here. I'm afraid it wouldn't work for you."

"Well then, will you take my picture?"

"Of course."

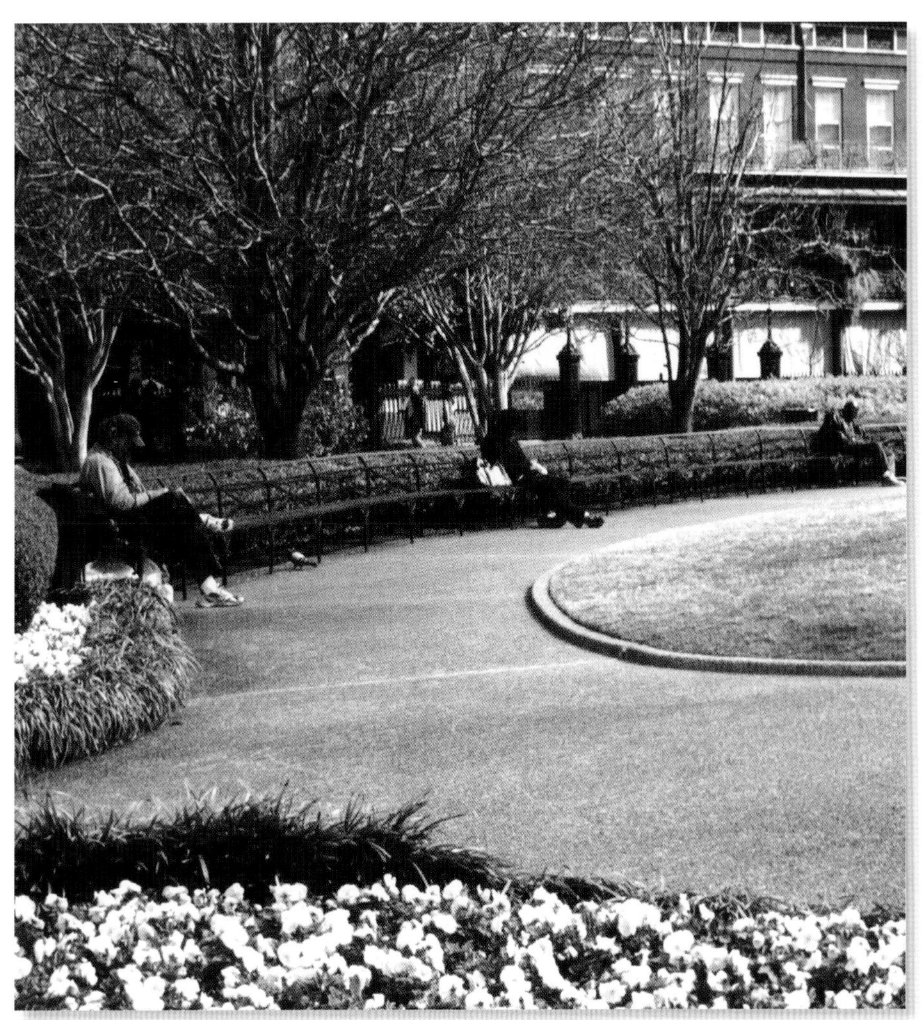

NEW ORLEANS, LOUISIANA

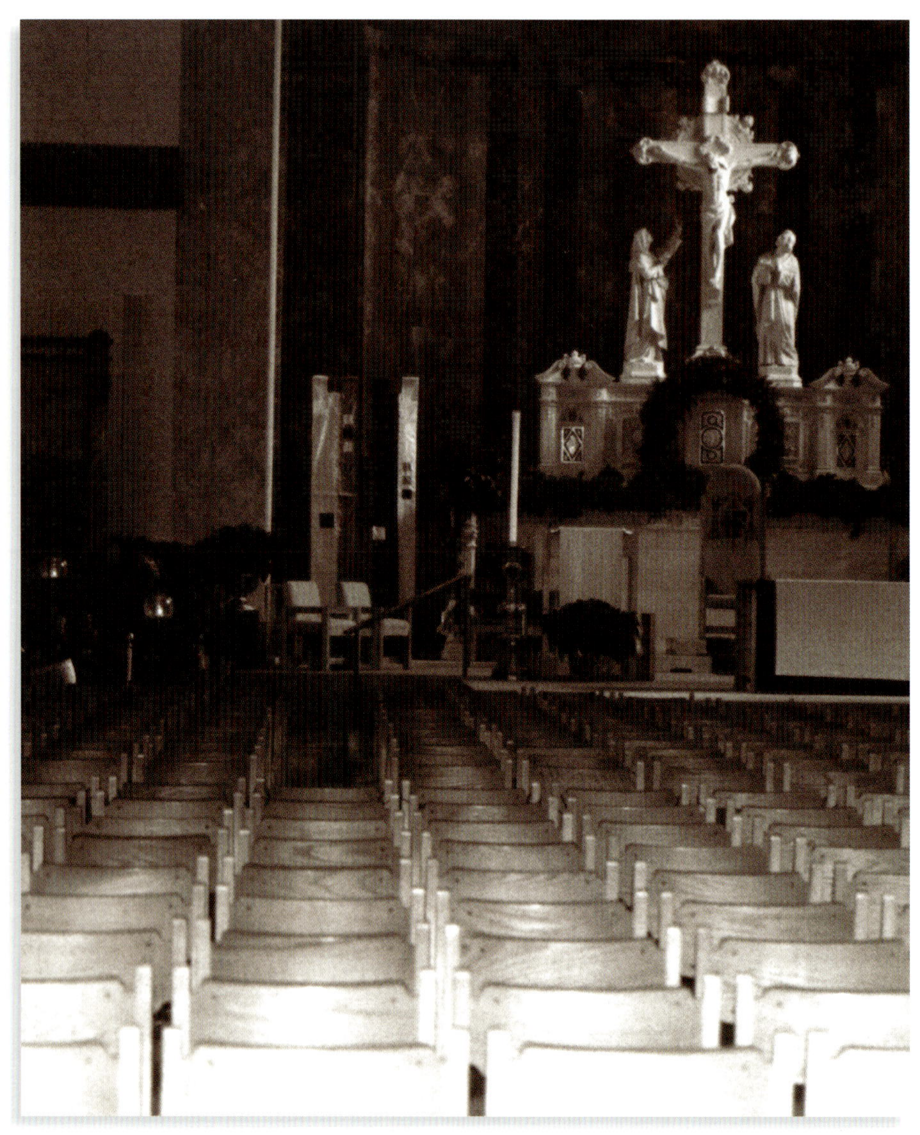

INDIANAPOLIS, INDIANA

Twelve people, three families, staying for a week in the small house with one bathroom. Now used as meeting rooms for the church, the house was deemed inadequate for the two priests who lived there in the past.

Next week, the three families would move to another house. It is an interdenominational ministry, so until they have their own places again, they will move every week.

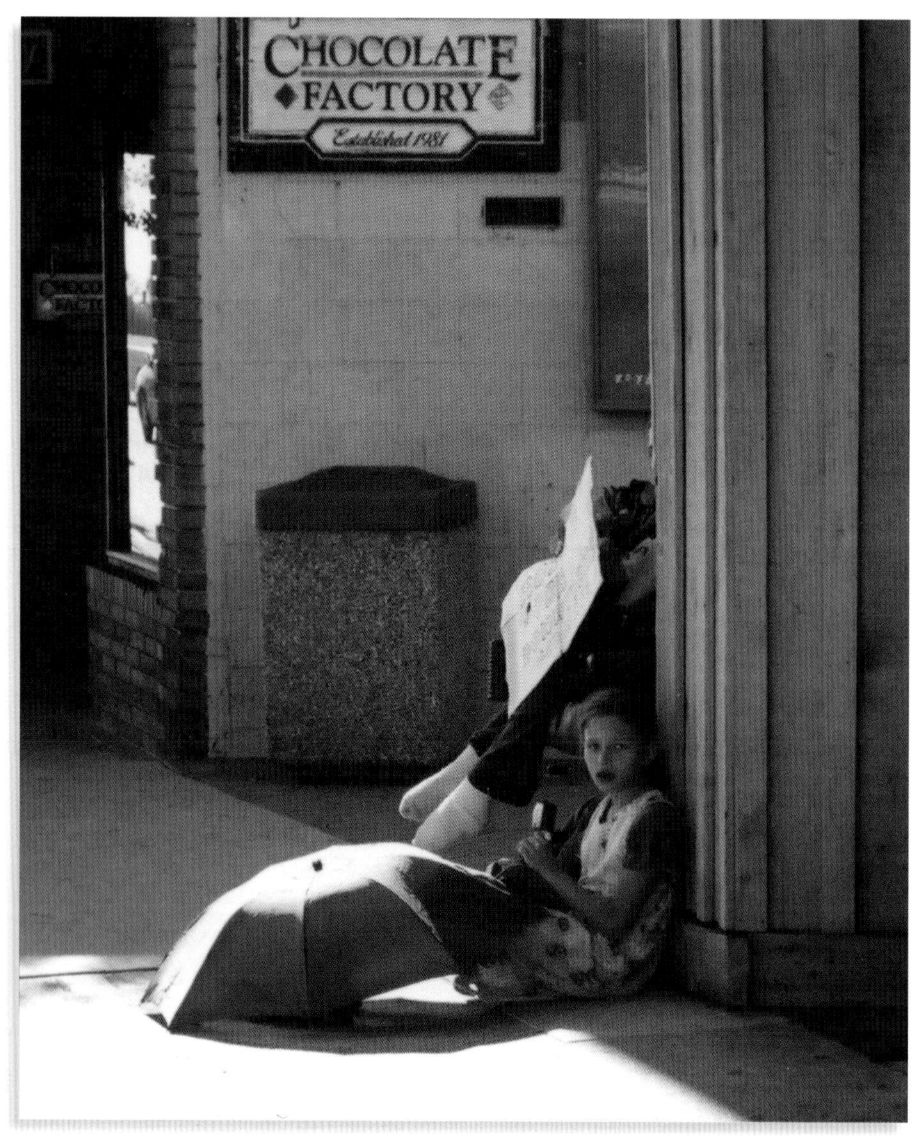

What must it be like to sit on the sidewalk with your mother behind you as you beg silently for money?

LAGUNA BEACH, CALIFORNIA

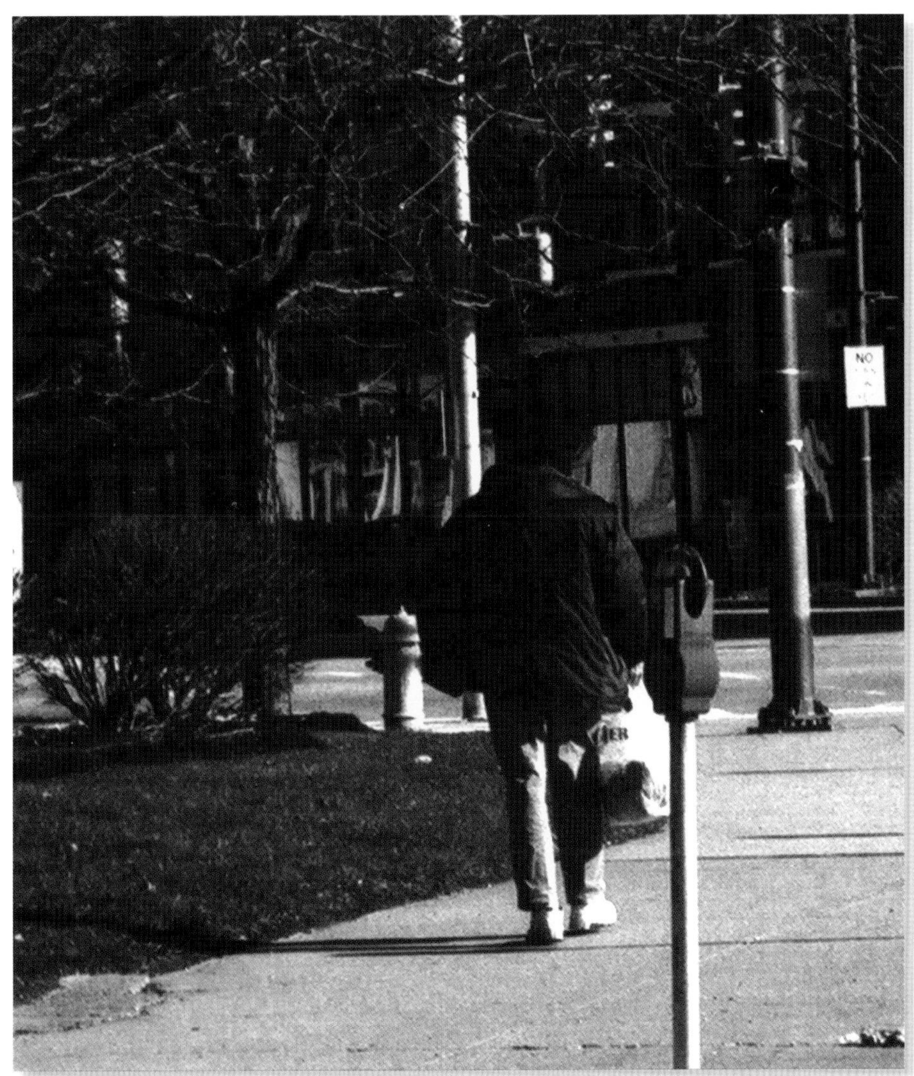

Are these the most tamed of souls or the most untamed?

Has life beaten them to the point where purpose has no place,

or are they living the most purposeful lives of us all,

totally in the now?

INDIANAPOLIS, INDIANA

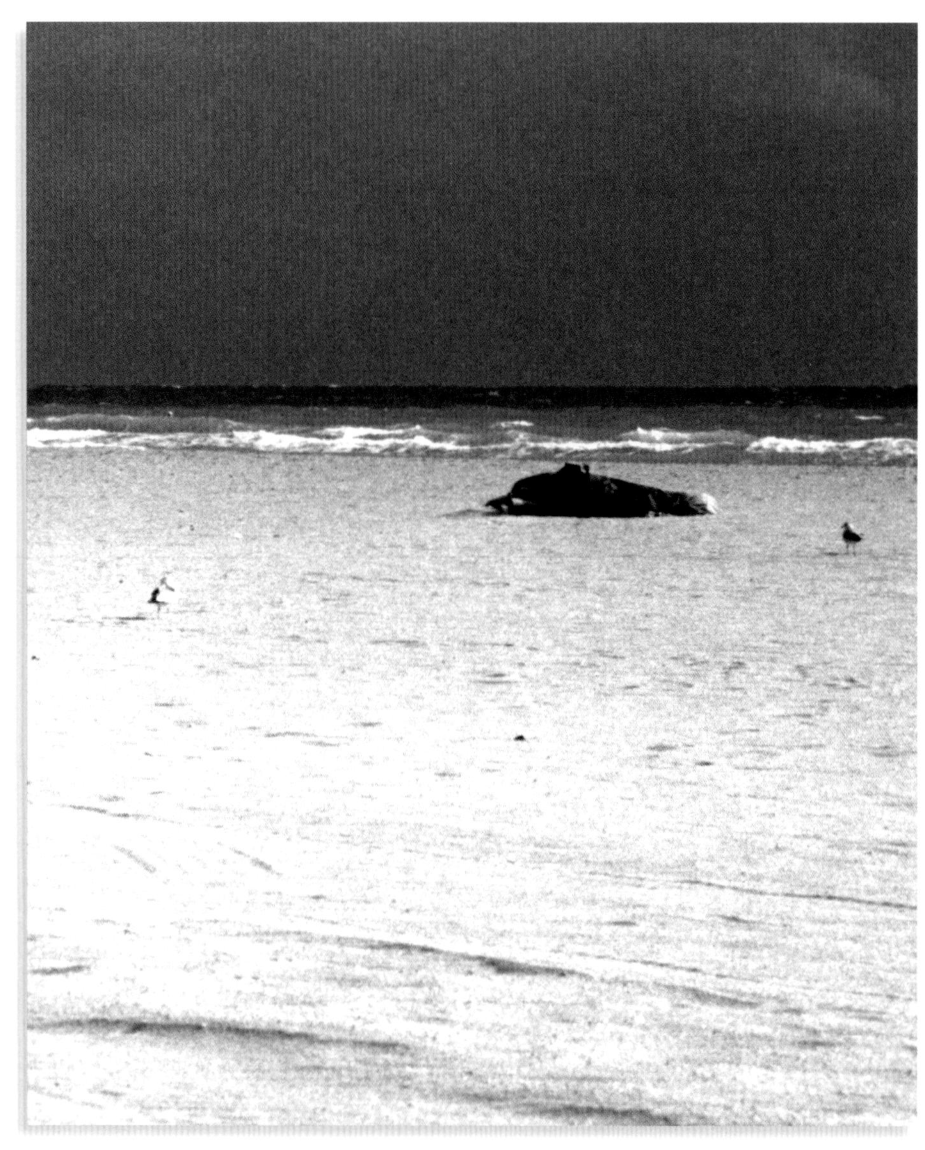

MIAMI, FLORIDA

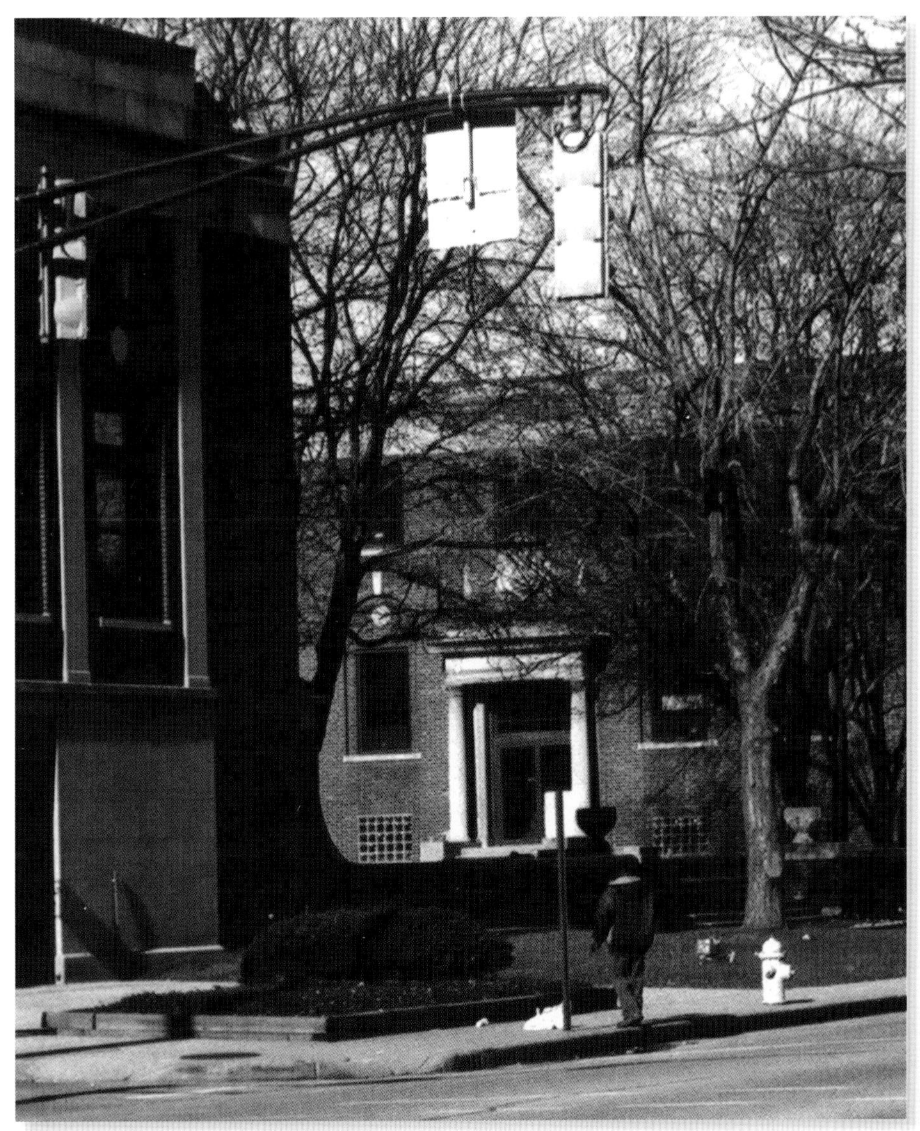

INDIANAPOLIS, INDIANA

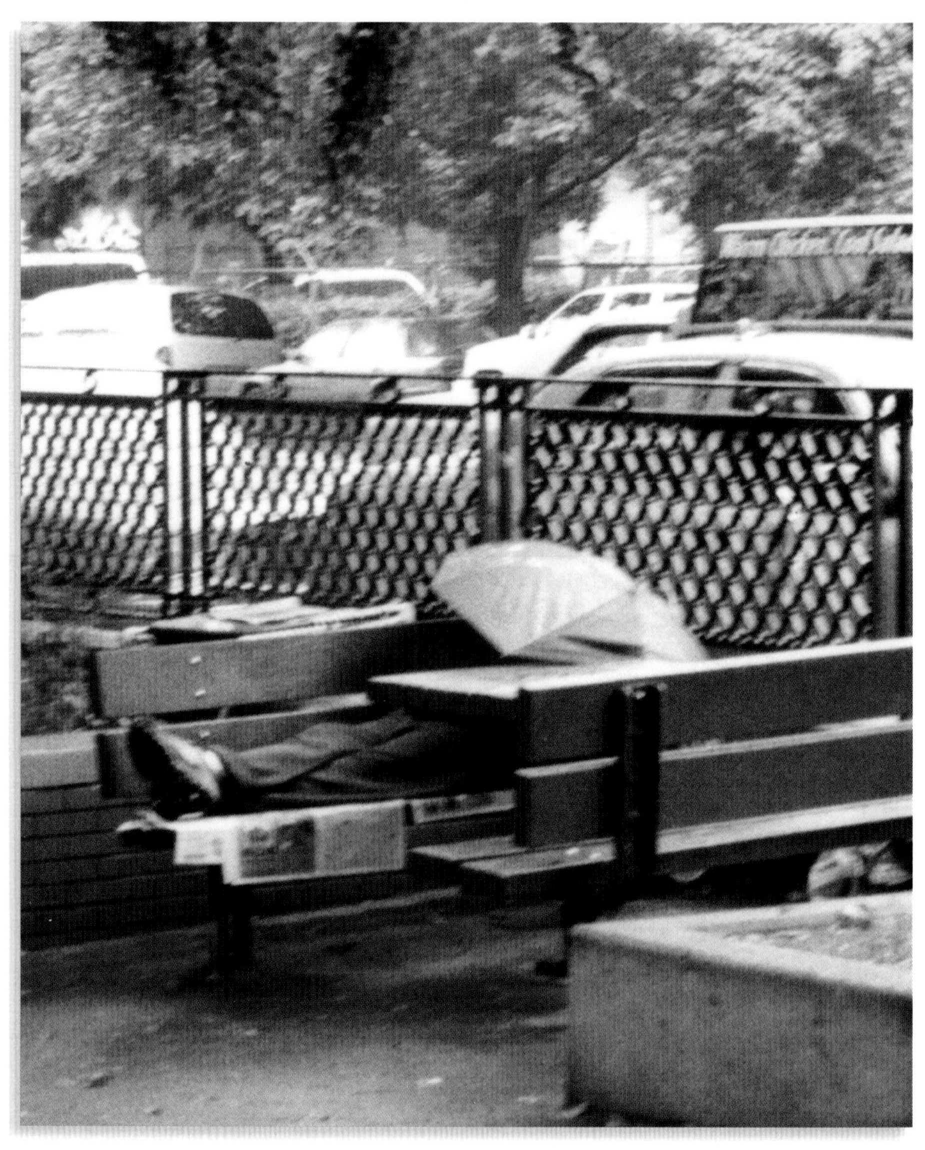

NEW YORK CITY, NEW YORK

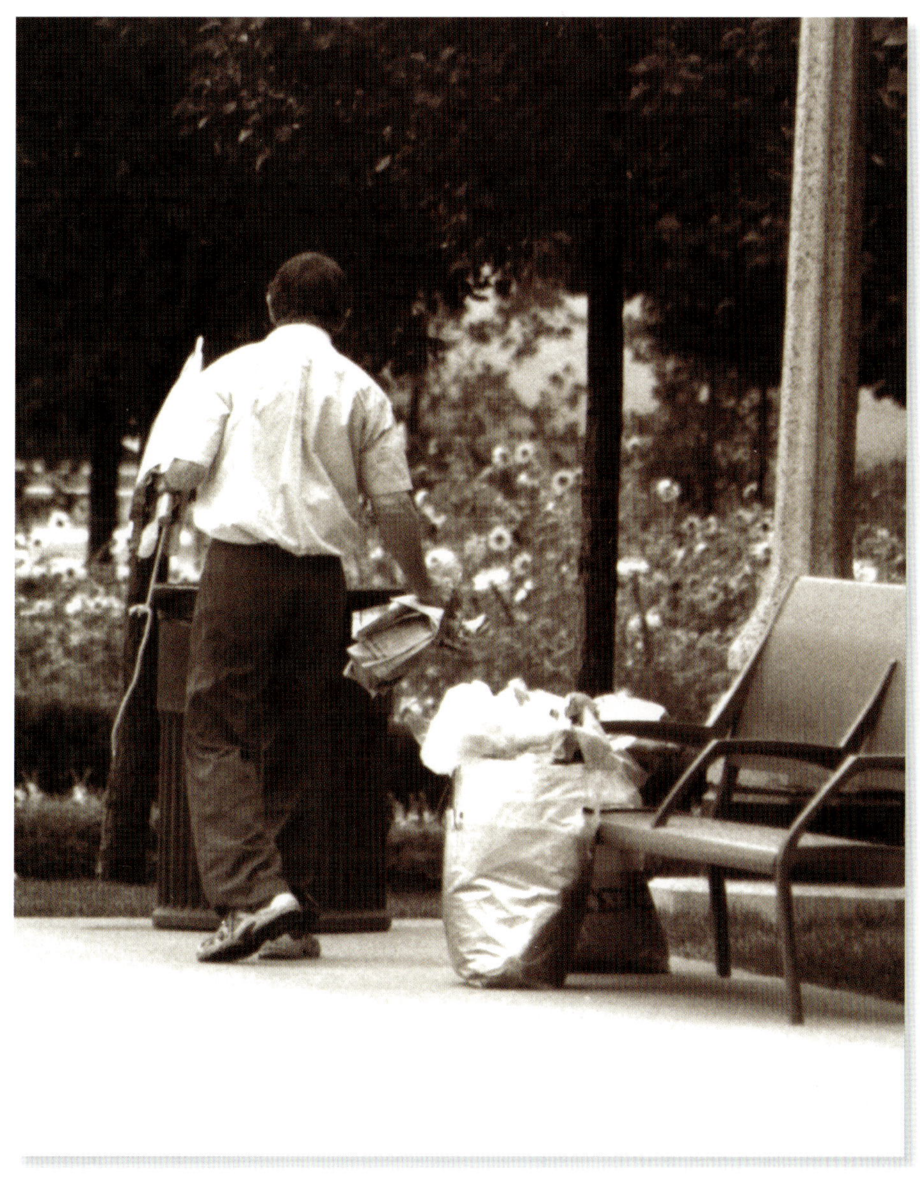

CHICAGO, ILLINOIS

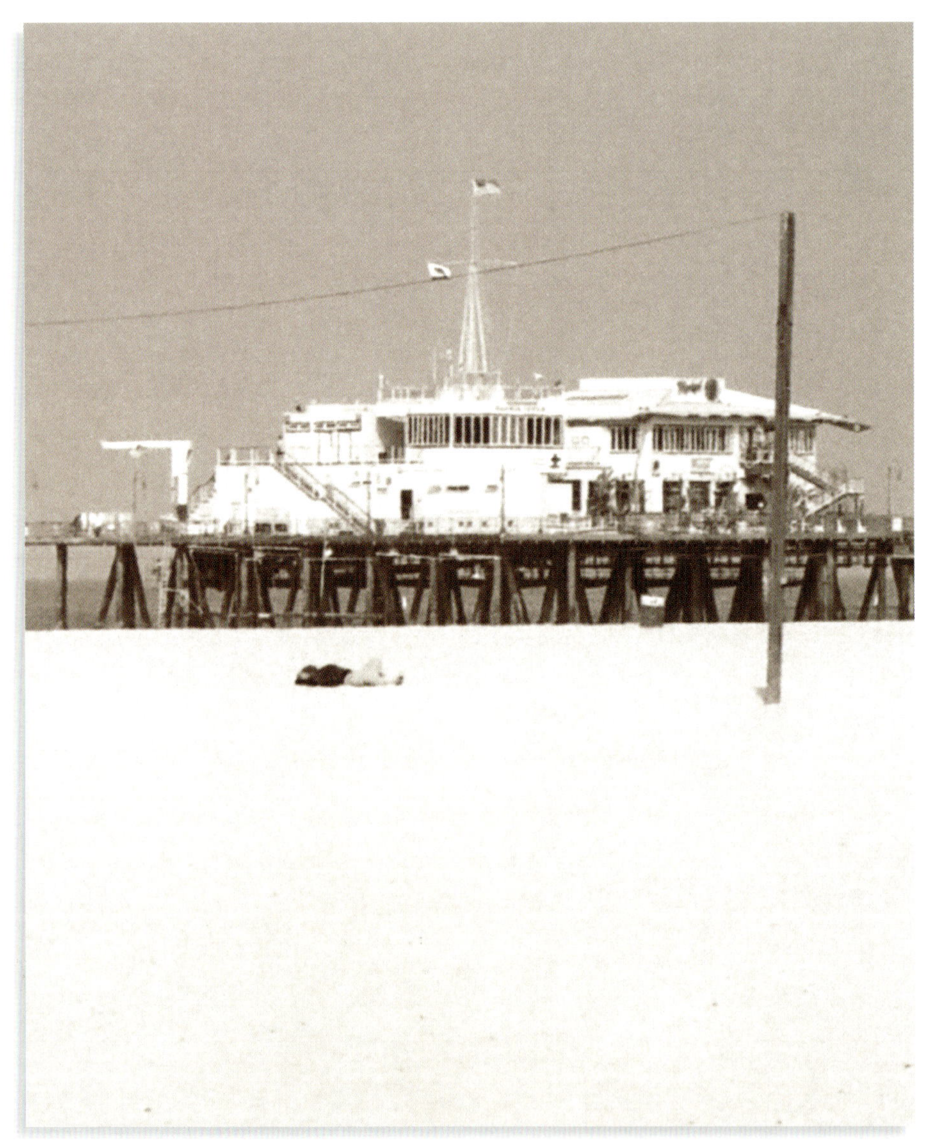

SANTA MONICA, CALIFORNIA

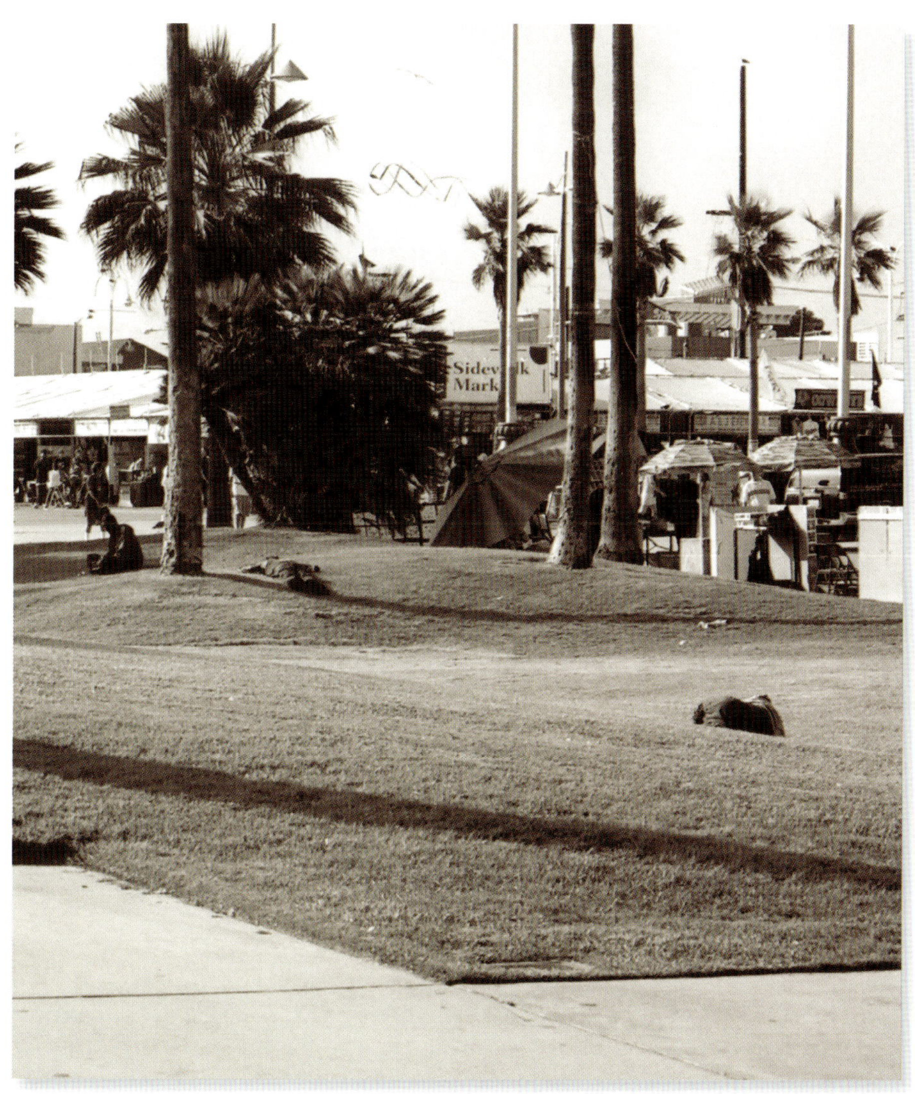

Dare we listen to the voices of the street? Dare we open our spirit to theirs? Or is this a danger beyond our responsibility, a problem beyond our scope?

VENTURA, CALIFORNIA

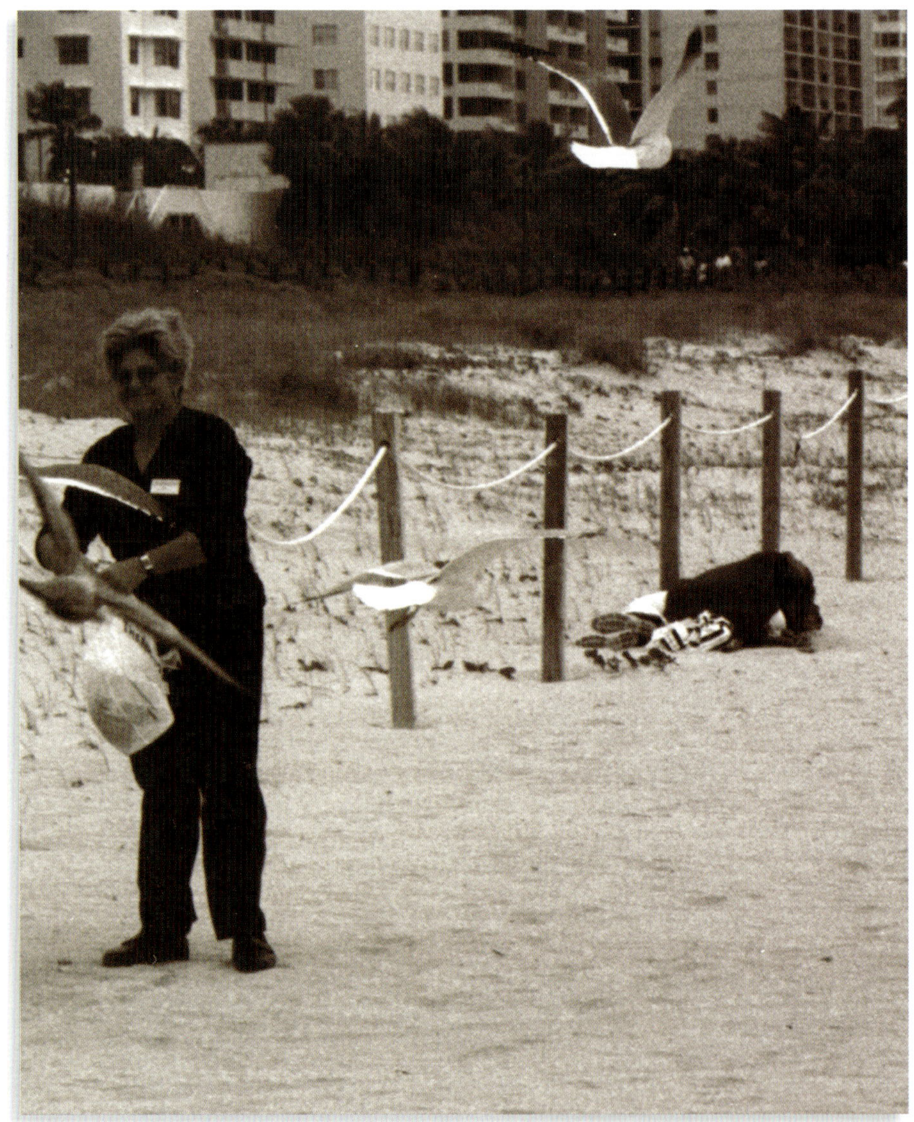

A radio talk show host described a town in Florida that had set up a soup kitchen program. It was quite successful and began to attract more and more hungry people. Then the city decided that was a problem… there were too many homeless people coming to their community.

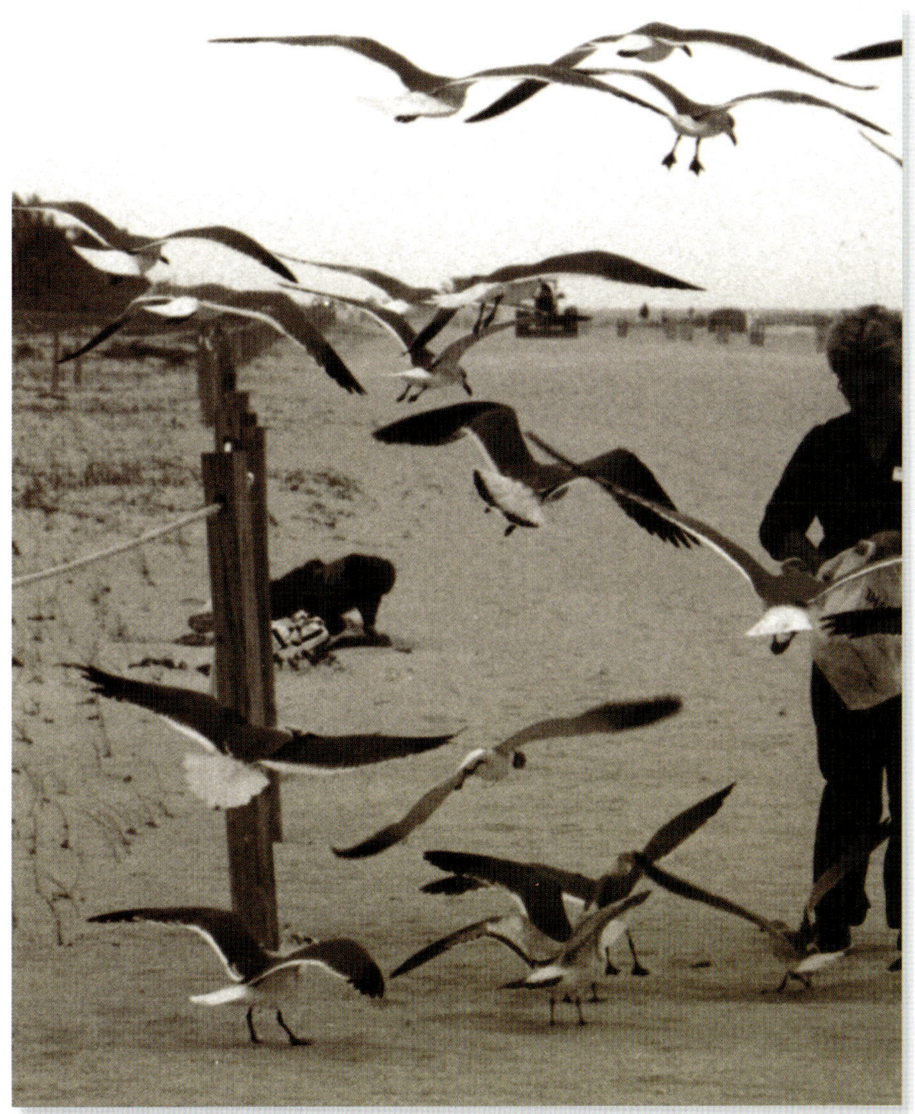

The radio host likened these people to sea gulls. They show up stinking, to eat, and just kind of spread crap all over the place.

Is that what this lady is thinking as she feeds the gulls on the beach, ignoring the sleeping person behind her?

Or are the gulls just more fun to feed?

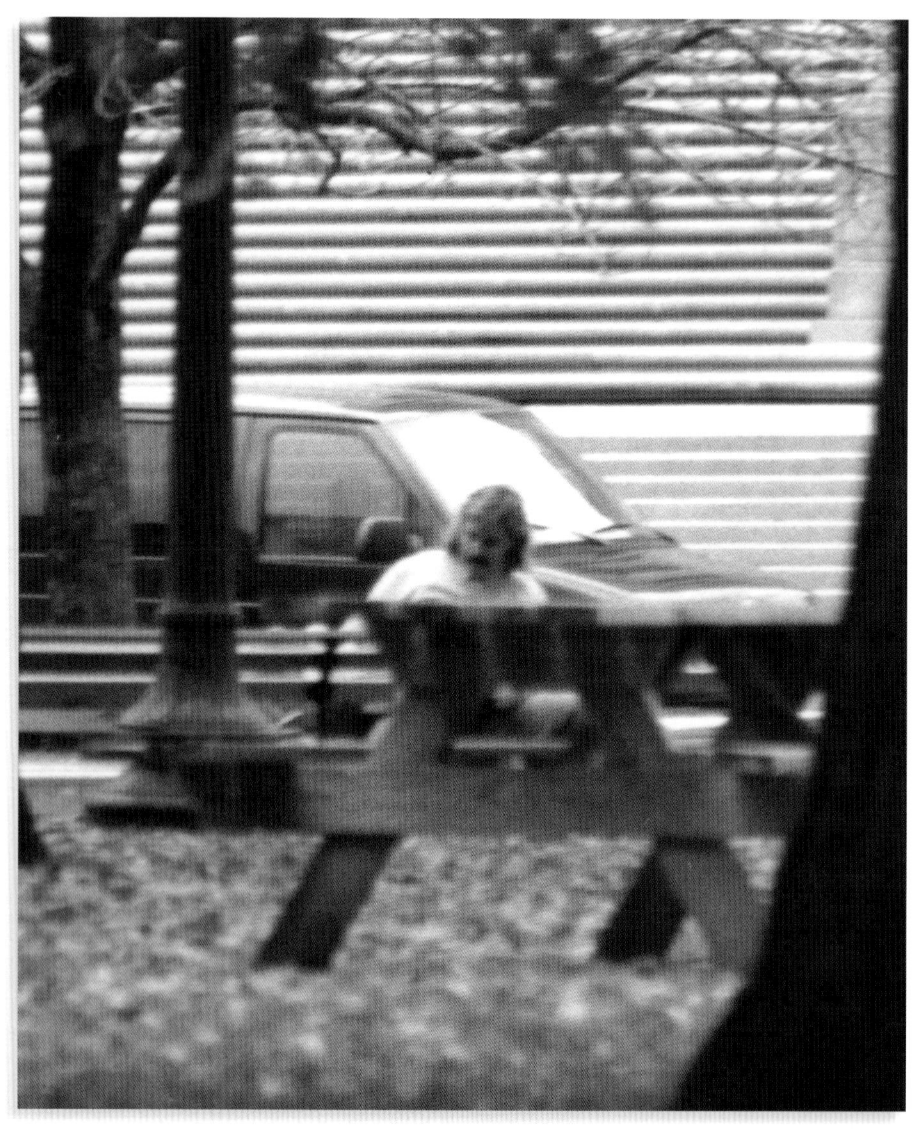

INDIANAPOLIS, INDIANA

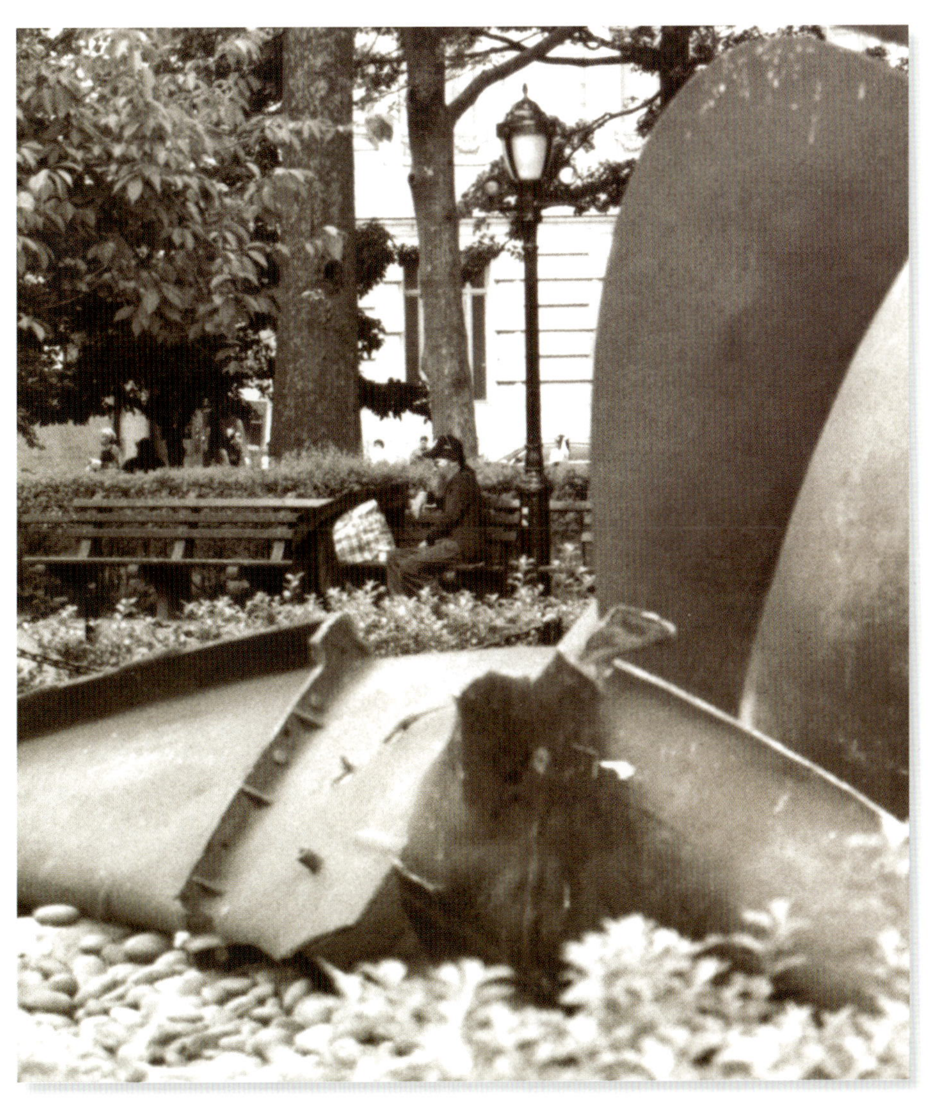

BATTERY PARK, NEW YORK CITY, NEW YORK

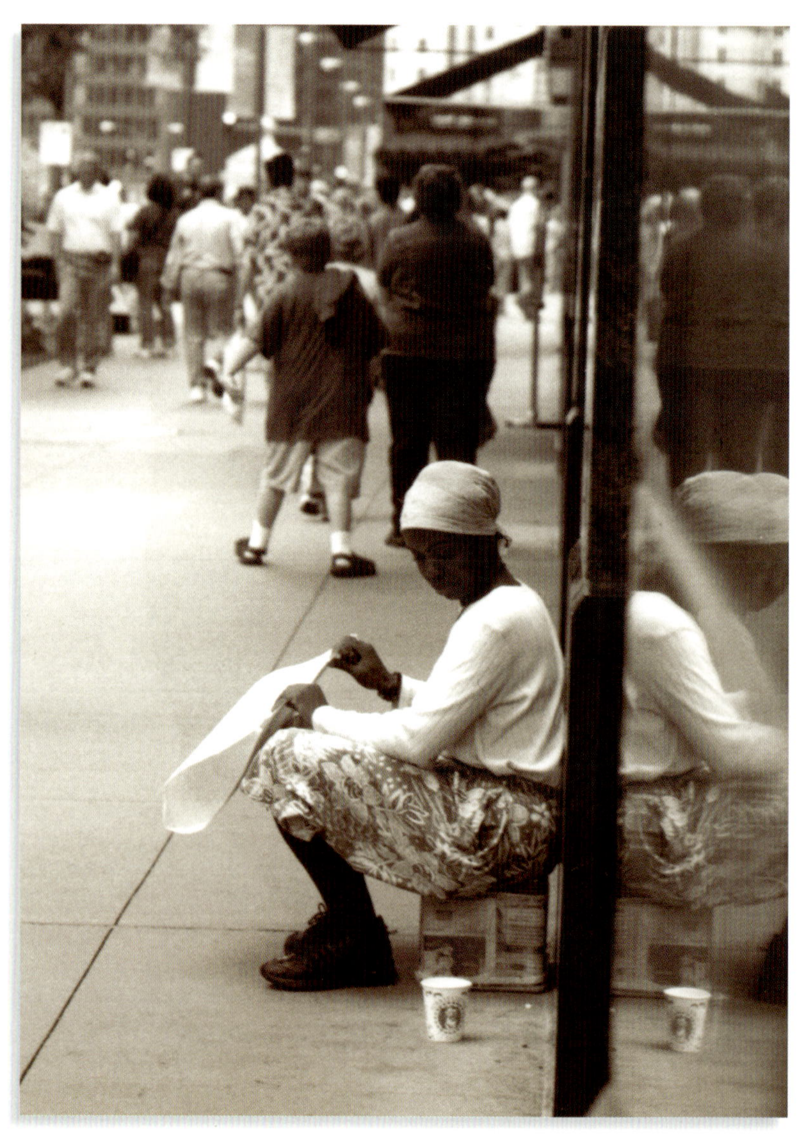

CHICAGO, ILLINOIS

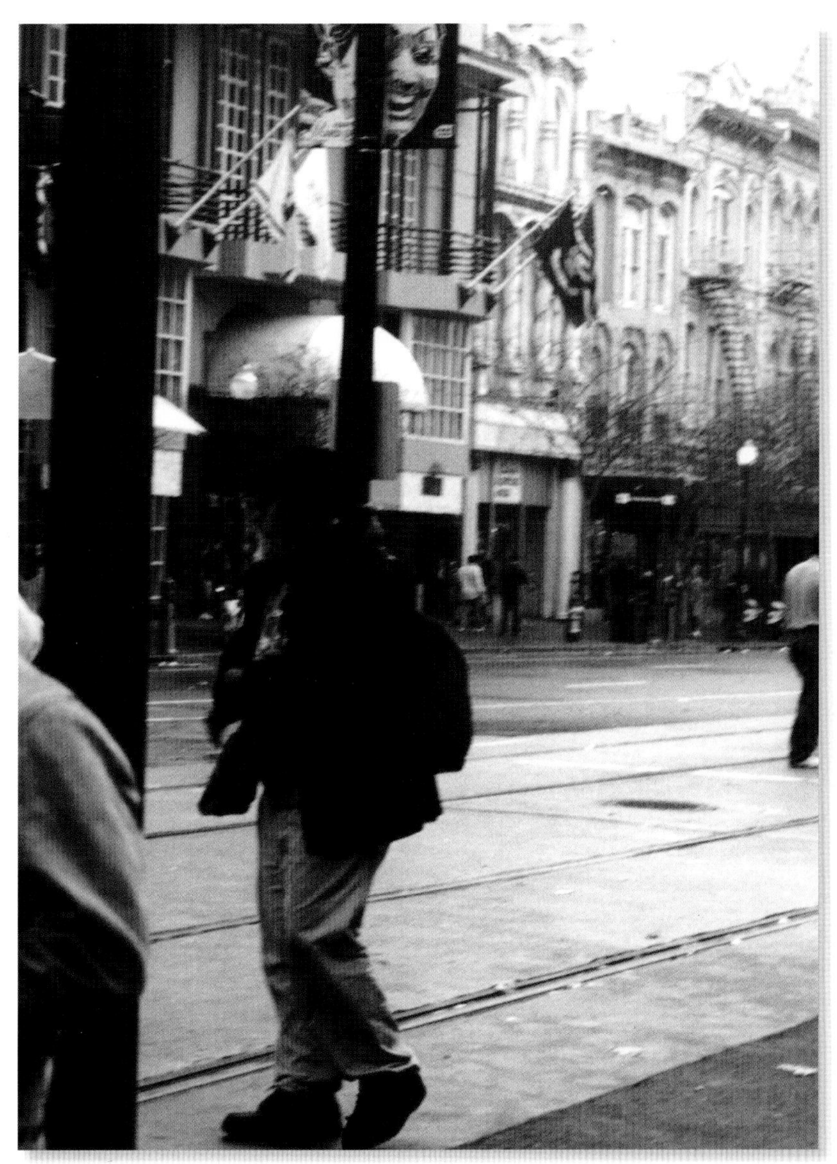

NEW ORLEANS, LOUISIANA

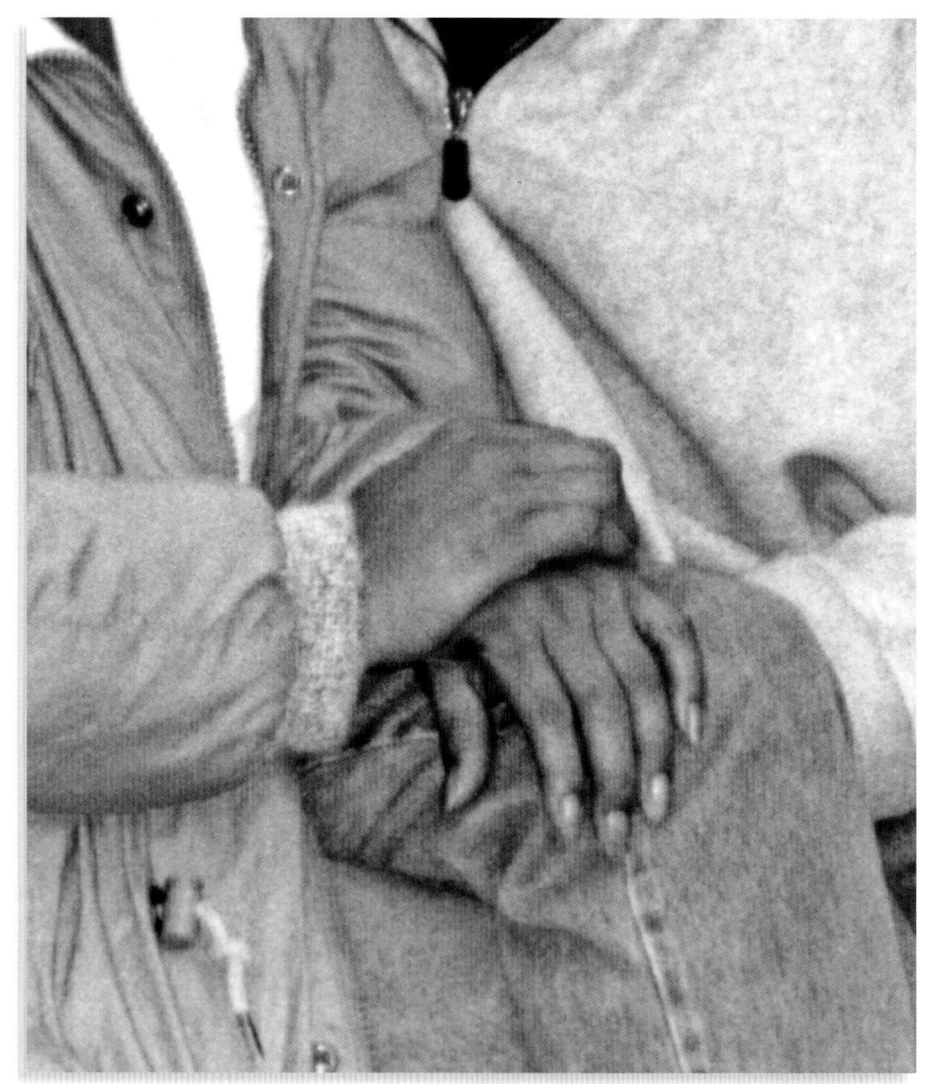

Love can be homeless.

INDIANAPOLIS, INDIANA

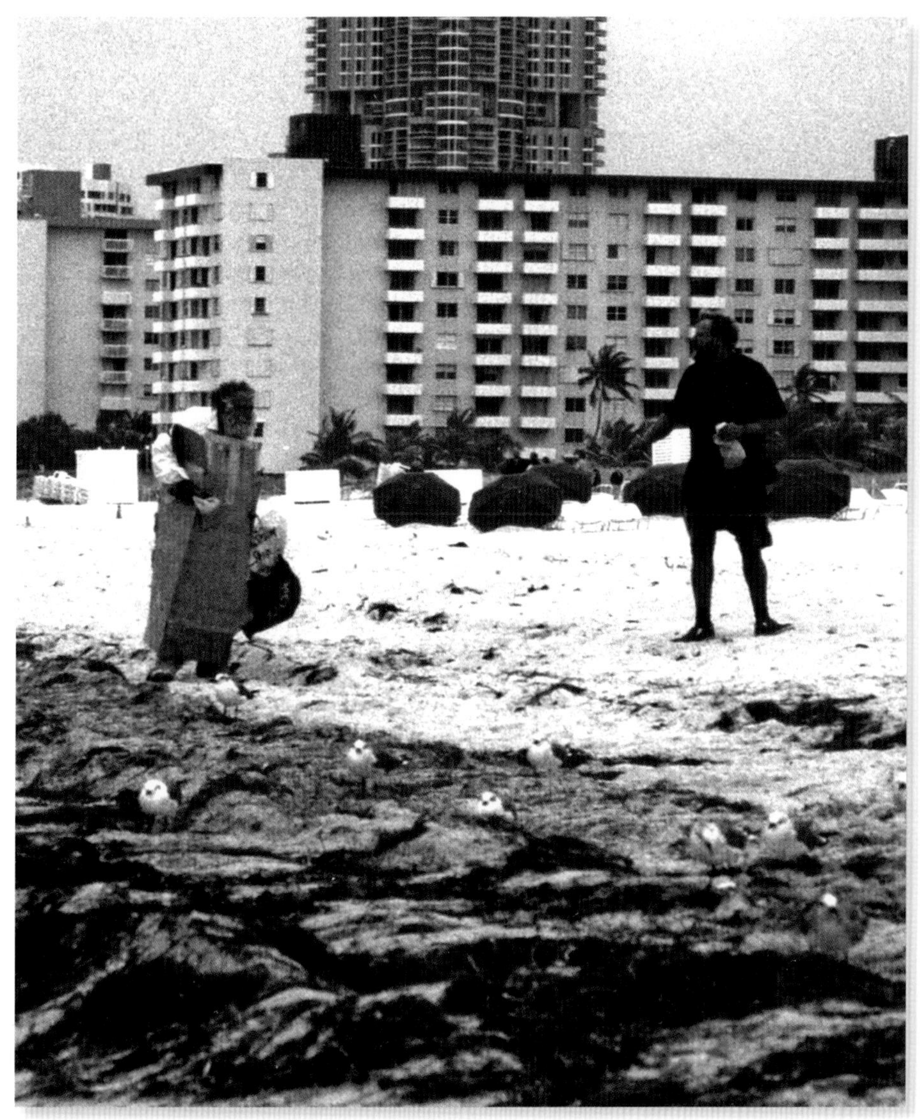

I asked, "Are they the neediest of us all or the freest of us all?" Her reply, "Don't try to romanticize them."

MIAMI, FLORIDA

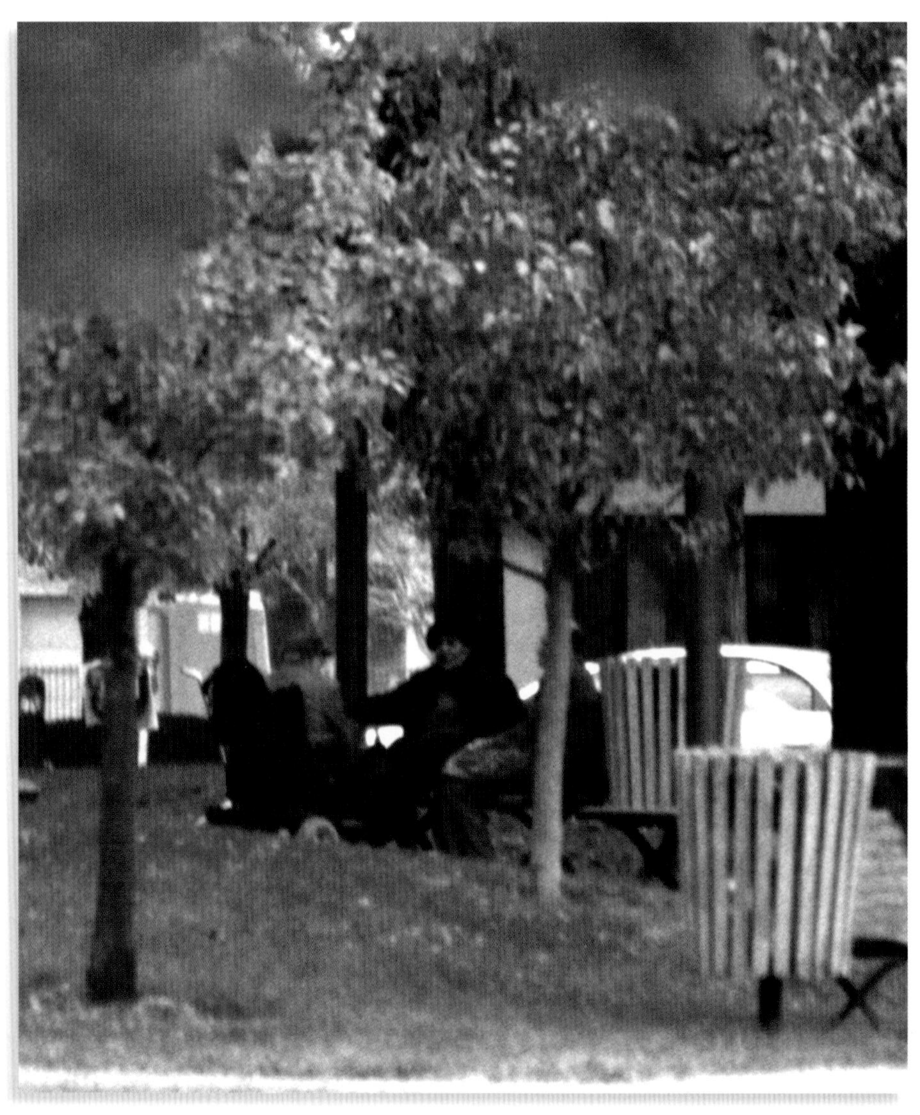

INDIANAPOLIS, INDIANA

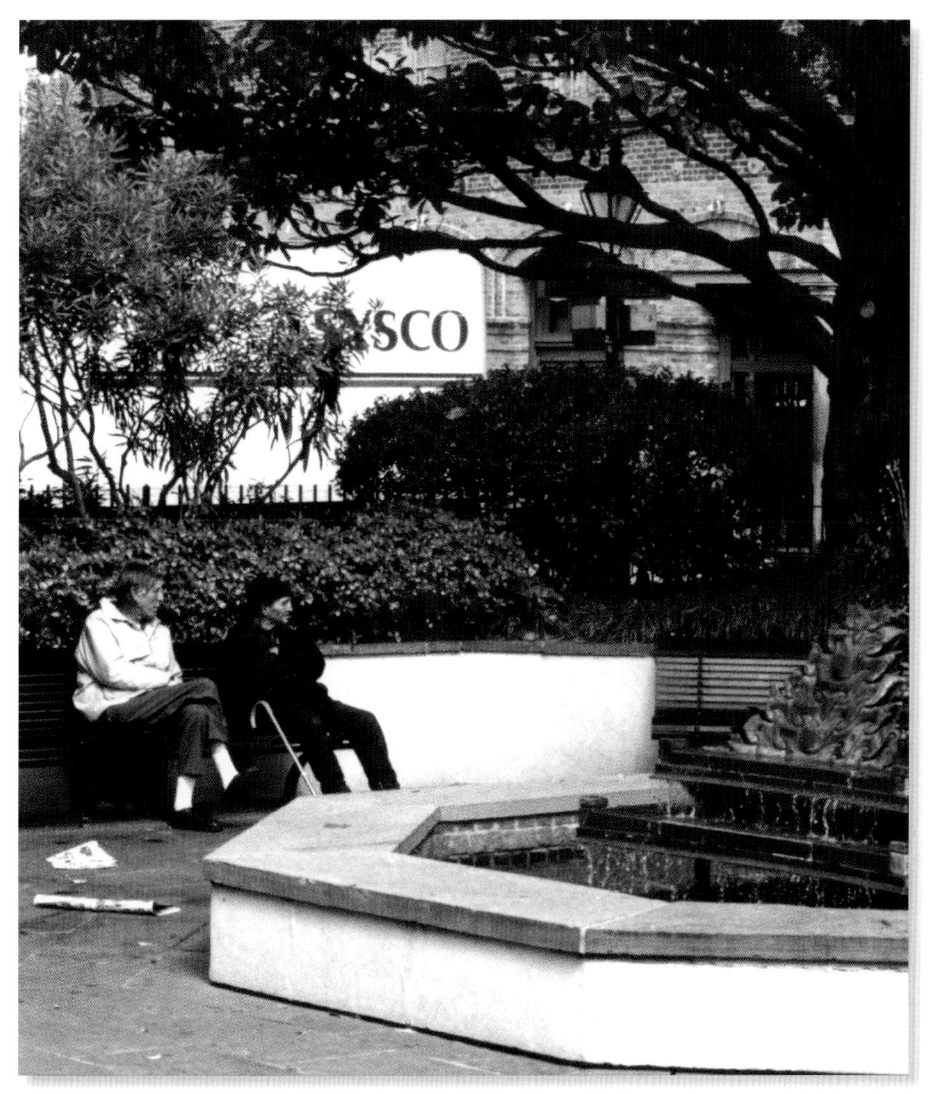

NEW ORLEANS, LOUISIANA

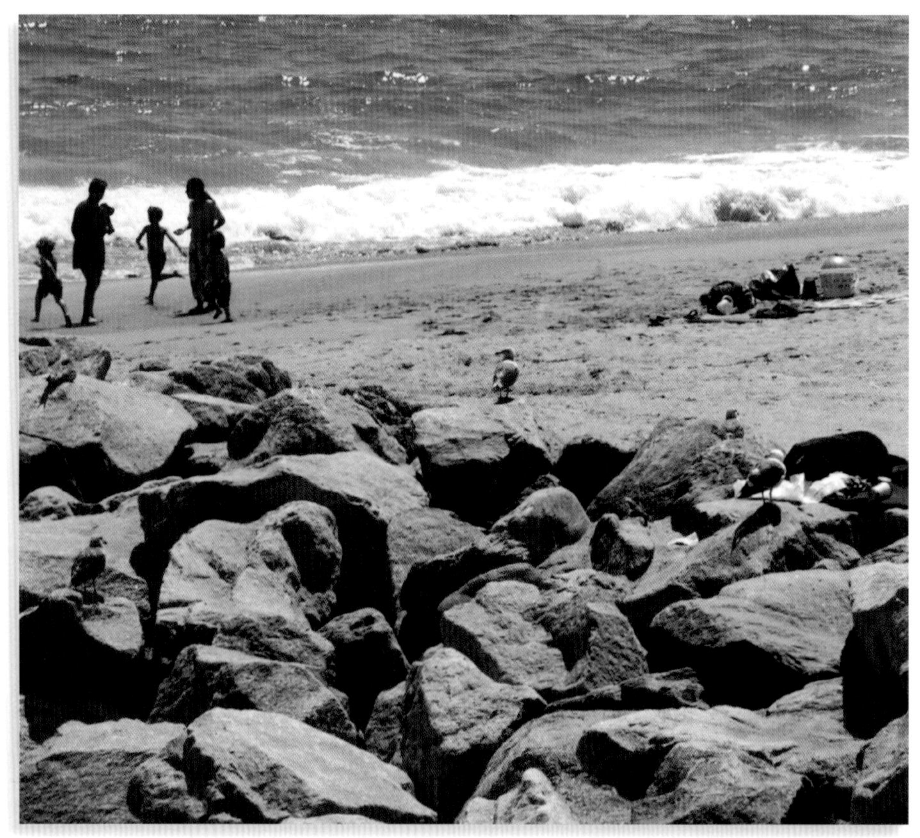

No One Sees Me.

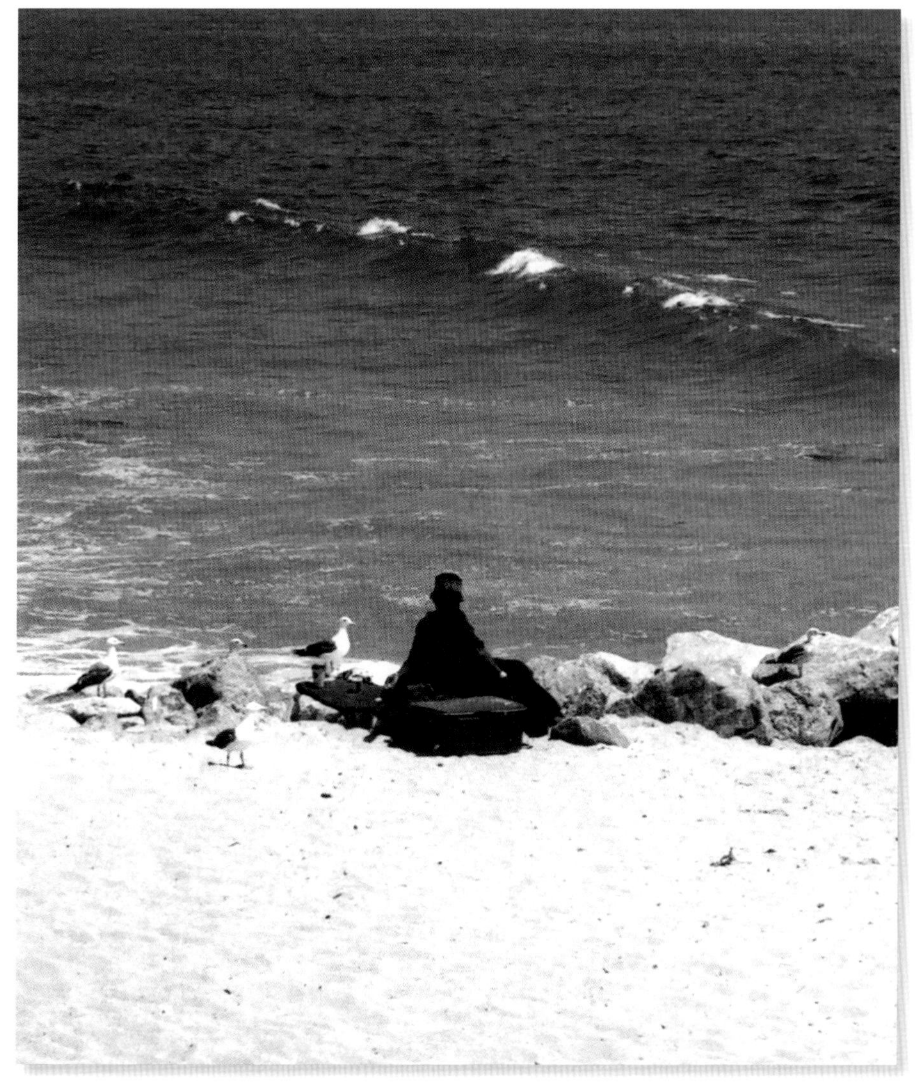

The end of Sunset Boulevard.

SANTA MONICA, CALIFORNIA